N ow from the author of *7 Approaches in Quantum* step guide to experiencin Quantum Consciousness. Dr. Steph. exercises to explore and experience the quantum approach to problem resolution. Designed to be done alone, in pairs, or in a group setting, this adventure takes us into a new frontier and pushes the envelope of even the most far reaching current psychological thought.

You will find *Quantum Consciousness* chockful—abundant with helpful exercises, insights often based on Dr. Wolinsky's own experiences, and techniques for altering awareness in situations where stuck patterns of perception have kept humanity in the caves of unenlightenment for far too long.

Fred Alan Wolf, Ph.D.,
author of *Taking the Quantum Leap, Star Wave, Parallel Universes, The Eagles Quest,* and co-author of *Space, Time and Beyond.*

Dr. Stephen Wolinsky has taken a giant step forward here into the trackless void of *Quantum Consciousness*—the world experienced as vibratory possibilities.

Nick Herbert, Ph.D.
author of *Quantum Reality* and *Faster Than Light*

This book breaks new ground in the kinds of experiences made possible by conscientiously doing the exercises detailed within. These exercises could very well result in major gains in self-knowledge and in therapeutic breakthroughs.

Robert Masters, Ph.D.
Director of Research, The Foundation for Mind Research.
Co-author of *Mind Games* and *The Varieties of Psychedelic Experience*

The paper used in this publication meets the minimum requirements
of American National Standard for Information Sciences—
Permanence of Paper for Printed Library Materials,
ANSI Z39.48-1984.

QUANTUM
CONSCIOUSNESS

The Guide to Experiencing
Quantum Psychology

Stephen Wolinsky, Ph.D.

contributor
Kristi L. Kennen, M.S.W.

BRAMBLE BOOKS

For information email:
info@bramblebooks.com

Library of Congress Cataloging-in-Publication Data

Wolinsky, Stephen.
    Quantum consciousness : the guide to experiencing quantum psychology / Stephen Wolinsky ; contributor, Kristi L. Kennen.
        p.   cm.
    Includes bibliographical references and index.
    ISBN 0-9626184-8-9 (pbk.) : $14.95
        1. Self-actualization (Psychology) 2. Centering (Psychology)—Problems, exercises, etc. 3. Meditations—Therapeutic use. 4. Psychic ability—Problems, exercises, etc. I. Kennen, Kristi L. II. Title.
BF637.S4W64 1993
158'.1—dc20   93-24895
                                  CIP

First Printing 1993

Printed in the United States of America

DEDICATION

To the memory of my teacher Nisargadatta Maharaj,
the ultimate de-programmer.

ACKNOWLEDGMENTS

Carl Ginsburg, Ph.D., Douglas Harding, Jack Horner, David Katzin, M.D., David and Carol Lange, Jerald H. Grimson (Illustrator), Baba Muktananda, Baba Nityananda, Robert Masters, Ph.D. and Jean Houston, M.D., whose format for a leaderless group in *Mind Games* was incorporated, Nisargadatta Maharaj, Bruce Carter and Donna Ross (word processing), Lynne Behnfield,(copy editor) and Karen Blicher, (general editor). Special thanks to Margaret O. Ryan whose re-write of the first 40 pages was invaluable, and Kristi L. Kennen, M.S.W. who co-authored Chapter 5.

Special thanks to all the workshop participants, sponsors, and trainees, who hung-out with me, and gave me trust and the benefit of the doubt.

THE AUTHOR

Stephen H. Wolinsky, Ph.D., began his clinical practice in Los Angeles, California in 1974. A Gestalt and Reichian therapist and trainer, he led workshops in Southern California. He was also trained in Classical Hypnosis, Psychosynthesis, Psychodrama/Psychomotor, and Transactional Analysis. In 1977 he journeyed to India, where he lived for almost six years studying meditation. He moved to New Mexico in 1982 to resume a clinical practice. There he began to train therapists in Ericksonian Hypnosis, N.L.P. and family therapy. Dr. Wolinsky also conducted year-long trainings entitled: Integrating Hypnosis with Psychotherapy, and Integrating Hypnosis with Family Therapy. Dr. Wolinsky is the author of *Trances People Live: Healing Approaches in Quantum Psychology®, The Tao of Chaos: Quantum Consciousness Volume II* and *The Dark Side of the Inner Child: The Next Step* (Bramble Books). He is the co-developer of Quantum Seminars™ and the founder of Quantum Psychology®. Along with Kristi L. Kennen, M.S.W., he founded the first Quantum Psychology Institute®.

TABLE OF CONTENTS

QUANTUM EXERCISES

FOREWORD

Dr. Stephen Wolinsky has created one of the most interesting and stimulating psychologies since Abraham Maslow.

Ever since I wrote my study of Maslow, *New Pathways in Psychology*, in 1970, I have been a fascinated spectator of the slow de-freudianization of psychology. First came Viktor Frankl's *existenz-psychologie*, which emerged from his experience in Nazi death camps, and was based on the recognition that man's mental and physical health depends upon his sense of purpose. At around the same time, English and American readers became aware of the Zurich school of existenz-psychologists, led by Ludwig Binswanger, who emphasized the need for the psychoanalyst to get 'inside' the patient's neurosis, and stop importing his own prejudices. The starting point of Assagioli's 'psychosynthesis' was the recognition that man possesses a central core of being, a 'self', and that by recognizing his own creative potentialities, man can develop 'towards the Superconscious.' Maslow also decisively rejected Freud's mechanistic vision of man, and spoke of 'higher ceilings of human consciousness.' For me, the essence of experiences', those sudden flashes of strength and sheer happiness that are characteristic of all healthy people. Carl Rogers recognized the central importance of self-esteem, an idea that was also ingeniously developed by Nathaniel Branden.

There is a sense in which all these developments are a return to the observation made by William James in a little book called *On Vital Reserves* (1900), in which he pointed out that 'the human individual...lives usually far within his limits; he possesses powers of various sorts which he habitually fails to use', and identifies man's central problem as 'an inveterate *habit* of inferiority to our full self.' So while Freud was trying to prove that man was far more helpless than we assume, James and his successors were trying to demonstrate that man is far *stronger* than he realizes, and that the cure of his neuroses depends upon him learning to recognize this.

In my own view, one of the most interesting of recent developments is the technique of 'focusing' developed by Eugene T. Gendlin. This consists basically of teaching the patient to look inside himself and to try to 'focus' the essence of his unhappiness and express it in words. While this clearly has something in common with Freud's 'talking cure', it is also a technique that comes naturally to every writer—particularly to the poet: learning to pour out his problems on paper, as to expel them from his system.

All of which demonstrates that there is no such thing as 'originality' in psychology. Psychology is, after all, the science of the human soul, and everyone who is capable of accurate observation will inevitably recognize the same fundamental truths.

What strikes me as so interesting about Stephen Wolinsky is that he began approaching these truths in the same spirit as so many of the 'religious Outsiders' I wrote about in my first book.[1] He admits to having been a 'workshop junkie', and to spending six years studying in India, and then another twelve years in meditation three times a day. It is obvious that, like St. Augustine, Jacob Boehme, George Fox, Blaise Pascal, Sri Ramakrishna, he found the issue of 'personal salvation' a matter of almost physical urgency. And eventually, his self-observation led him to recognize that 'the witness not only *witnesses and is mindful* of what passes through the mind and body, but it is also the *creative source* of it.' This is easy enough to grasp if you simply rub your eyes vigorously, then close the eyelids and try to *observe* the coloured shapes that float around. Your own observation changes the shapes as you try to look at them. Husserl called his effect 'intentionality.' Stephen Wolinsky prefers to speak of Heisenberg's Uncertainty Principle, whereby the observation of sub-atomic events is influenced by the observer. And this in turn led him to develop a technique for *'pulling beyond the creating observer',* and achieving what he calls the 'no-state state.' He came to recognize the basic truth of Bohm's notion of an 'implicate order' which lies behind phenomena, and which forms an 'unbroken wholeness which connects us all.'

Now what Dr. Wolinsky has uncovered here is the basic mystical experience. It is described, for example, in Franklin Merrel-Wolff's *Pathways Through to Space*: 'Then with eyes open...I abstracted the subjective moment—the 'I AM' or Atman element—from the totality of the objective consciousness manifold. Upon this I focused. Naturally, I found what, from the relative point of view, is Darkness and Emptiness. *But I Realized It as Absolute Light and Fullness and that I was That.*' And this produced in Merrel-Wolff what he calls the 'ambrosia quality', a feeling of pure joy and freedom that lasted for days.

So it could be said that the real problem of psychotherapy is to uncover the deepest level of one's own identity, and to recognize 'That thou art' 'Tat tvam asi' The result is a sense of sheer ecstasy and relief, freedom from the 'false self' that has entangled us like a boa constrictor. Ramakrishna experienced this feeling when he started to commit suicide by plunging a sword into his breast. Even Graham Greene, one of the gloomiest writers of our time, experienced something very similar when he played Russian roulette with a revolver and the hammer clicked on an empty chamber. But clearly this method is not to be recommended for general use.

Then how *can* it be done? This is where Dr. Wolinsky reveals the result of his twelve years of self-observation. He has devised a series of exercises—and these form the substance of this remarkable book—to enable any intelligent person to do 'work on himself' and to achieve results.

One very basic observation is that all our mental states consist basically of forms of energy. We regard some forms—pleasure, freedom—as good, and others—misery, guilt—as bad. But to recognize them simply as forms of energy is to abstract the 'false you' from the situation, and to remove the 'double bind.' In this respect, I particularly recommend Chapter VIII—'The Living Void', and the exercise called 'Einstein's Riddle', in which the conflict (in this case, whether to stay in a relationship or abandon it) is envisaged as particles in space, and then the space is seen as being of the same substance as the particles (as Einstein has said.) The result: 'the conflict disappears.'

What is so refreshing about Wolinsky is the sense of a brilliant mind enjoying its ability to solve problems. He is frank about his own insights and how they came to him; he speaks with the openness of a man who has nothing to hide. So quite apart from the exercises, I found that the book itself is an exhilarating and therefore therapeutic experience. Responding to Wolinsky's zest as he grapples with problems, the reader begins to run ahead of him and experience a sense of his own freedom—what Buckminster Fuller meant when he commented: 'I seem to be a verb.'

Every psychotherapy is an attempt to 'map the soul.' Analogies like Heisenberg's principle are simply a form of 'co-ordinate system' that enables us to take our bearings. William James preferred to start from the analogy of vital reserves, seeing the soul as a kind of battery that can get flat. Gurdjieff preferred the analogy of sleep and the war against sleep. Frankl saw it as a problem of 'the law of reverse effort.' What I find exciting about Wolinsky is that he has proved once again that a good basic 'co-ordinate system' can enable us to get to grips with the problem, and produce that healthy sense of freedom, of the power of the human mind to solve *any* problem. Like James, Frankl, Maslow, Rogers and Assagioli, he has found a new and highly original way of making us aware of one of the most paradoxical truths about human reality; that to say: 'I have freedom' is less accurate than to say: 'I *am* freedom.'

Colin Wilson

---

[1] *The Outsider,* 1956.

PROLOGUE

Upon my return from India in 1982, I began to teach workshops in my living room. These small groups ranging in size from eight to sixteen participants were the first step in the development of Quantum Psychology®. Much of this text also appeared in my doctoral thesis. As time went on, the workshops expanded and synthesized other schools and as well as psychological and spiritual disciplines to make the Quantum context experiential. I felt then, and still do now, that the ideal would be to teach approaches to working with oneself and others, so that people could organize their own informal groups. Ultimately in this way people could become their own teachers.

This book is limited in scope, since Quantum Psychology® contains an elaborate system of exploration that takes fifteen days of training to complete. The text was designed, however, to present over 80 exercises and contemplations to stimulate and explore oneself, in whatever setting you decide on. Some people are doing the work on their own, while others have found it more valuable to create their own leaderless study group that meets in someone's home every week or every other week. This way of *rotating* the facilitators' role, and having each person take a turn guiding the group through Quantum exercises, processes, and sharing seems to be most effective, and probably the one I would recommend.

Many workshop participants have said to me that the Quantum style of work opens up so many different windows of understanding that, often, they lack a context or group to talk it over with, which they felt was needed. Certainly it can help to provide support while making certain internal changes.

Quantum Psychology® really asks the reader to *practice* and do the exercises and contemplations, rather than just read them. Quantum Psychology® is not a spectator sport. I have tried to include exercises and contemplations that were explainable and do-able in the context of the book. If one exercise doesn't fit or work move on to another one—it *doesn't* mean you are less evolved, or not ready, it means it doesn't fit for you so move on to the next one. The parts of the system presented here are meant to embrace and be added to whatever "work" you are already doing with yourself, and is surely not meant as the *only way* or the *"cure all."* The exercises work best when done with an open mind, putting your definitions of the world, both inner and outer, *aside*, using a "What if this is true," "Suppose," or "Let's look at this as a possibility" attitude. After each exercise is completed, if done in a group context, numerous meanings will be generated from the group. Actually, there truly is no one meaning to the exercises—just doing them and exploring is enough.

I hope you enjoy the process as much as I did, or shall I say, "I hope it *is* as good for you, as it was for me."

With Love,
Your brother,
Stephen

ONE

AROUSING
THE GIANT

For as long as I can remember, my greatest wish was to be able to answer the question *"Who am I?"* I pursued this goal for over two decades, trampling through every major and minor discipline of Western psychology, Eastern meditation, and even Quantum Physics, as well as side trips into the drugs and "free" sexuality of the 1960's.

By 1976 I had had my chakras balanced, restored my body to its orgasmic best through Reichian therapy, sat in the Gestalt "hot seat," reenacted traumas of my childhood in psychodrama, explored the sub-personalities and ego states of Psychosynthesis and Transactional Analysis, learned over a hundred meditation techniques, been rebirthed, and chanted the name of God in several different languages.

Still I felt incomplete. I had no calming sense of knowing who I was, I had not found an experience of myself that was permanent, I could not point to a changeless Self. I kept being different selves that changed all the time as I went into different emotional states. One moment I liked myself, the next I didn't. One day I was contented with my life, the next day I was restless.

After so many years of being a workshop junkie, I met an Indian guru. He, I was told, not only knew who he was, but could somehow transmit this knowingness to me, so that eventually I would reach a state of liberation and freedom. Of course, no upstanding workshop junkie could turn down such an opportunity—particularly since it only cost $50.

Before long I was a devotee, still wondering when I would get enlightened, when I would finally "find myself" and know the answer to my lifelong question "Who am I?"

I spent almost six years in a monastery in India, chanting, working, and meditating my way through clouds of emotional pain, finding no answer.

Then, through personal contact with Nisargadatta Maharaj, another Indian Teacher, I began to discover who or what I was *not*: I was not my mind...I was not my thoughts...I was not my emotions...I was not anything that was knowable. I was the *witness* of all these things that came and went but which were not me. I later learned that this approach of discovering who you are by first experiencing who you are not was a path unto itself. A practical analogy for it might be: peeling away the layers of an onion. What most of us didn't realize when we began such a process was that after all the layers of the "onion" were peeled away—*nothing* remained. More on that later.

For the next five years, back in the States, I meditated three to five hours daily and resumed my investigations of Western psychotherapeutic methods. Ericksonian hypnosis and family therapy became added ingredients in my internal synthesis. By late 1985 I realized I was falling into a chronic state of depression. Not only had I not discovered who I was, but I began to perceive all models of psychotherapy, yoga, and spiritual disciplines as just that—*models*. They were belief systems—pictures, stories, renditions of the truth—but not *the truth*. If they had contained *the truth*, I would certainly not be depressed because, after all, "I believed" that "the truth" frees one of all pain.

I re-entered psychotherapy and bodywork as a client again on almost a daily basis. There were periods of time in which I was receiving seven hours of bodywork and several hours of "regular" therapy each week, in addition to my heavy meditation practice. I left no stone unturned, but still felt no inner resolution.

I was a student of Buddhism and Buddha had said that the self does not exist. But I had said, "Sure, right, the self does not exist, but now "*I*" have to meditate, "*I*" have to process these feelings, "*I*" have to work on myself..."*I*" have to surrender..."*I*" have to stop resisting"...and on and on.

After meditating several hours a day for many years, I could get into a peaceful space, a quiet void, but after I stopped meditating, the effect would last, if I was lucky, only a couple of hours. Then my mind would come back and I would start feeling uncomfortable, irritable, angry, or whatever, run back to my meditation, and witness the same stuff all over again.

In 1986 I realized that my Eastern teachings were overlooking a major aspect of the observer or witness: the witness not only *witnesses and is mindful* of what passes through the mind and body, but it is also the *creative source* of it.

In other words, the witness or observer of the mind (thoughts, feeling, emotions and associations), not only witnesses thoughts or emotions, but somehow instantaneously creates that which it witnesses. What I mean by this is that a thought called "I don't like myself" appears "as if" it had always been there and had a life of its own. In reality, however, in a mysterious way the observer creates the thought, through the act of observation; observation was the creative vehicle of the observer. Stated more simply, in order for the observer to have a job called observing, it must create something to *observe*.

It was at this point that Heisenberg's Uncertainty Principle (more about this later) became something I could *experience*, not just think about. In essence, it states that all reality is *observer-created*. Now I actually experienced that I was first *creating* the thoughts that I then observed or witnessed while meditating. My rediscovery of Heisenberg's work on an *experiential* level reopened the field of quantum physics to me and led me further into developing the system of Quantum Psychology. I began *rereading* all the books I could lay my hands on. The implications of quantum physics swirled around the Eastern teachings in my mind as I began to sense how each system was pointed toward a common "truth" of the underlying unity of everything. I also began to understand how quantum physics could be integrated with Western psychology to "speed up" the resolution of problems both I and my clients were experiencing.

I worked very diligently for the next year-and-a-half to understand and *experience* how my reality was observer-created. One day I was sitting, watching my observer-created realities appear and disappear, watching the observer come and go out of my awareness, when I realized that I was also *beyond* the observer and my observer-created reality. The observer in me, it seemed, arose with each new creation, as though the two, observer and its creation (i.e., thought or feeling) were instantaneously related. And since "I" could witness not only my thoughts, but myself witnessing my thoughts, I realized that something must extend beyond the confines of the observer-creation dyad. Gradually I began to feel no longer bound by the continual comings and goings of the observer who was creating, becoming, experiencing, and finally, observing, each new "reality." There was a "me-beyond-observer-created-realities" that existed in what I called a "no-state state" that felt open, empty, and freeing. It was a state I could easily re-enter by pulling my attention away from the thoughts and focusing on myself, the one behind the thoughts. Often, in meditation, one tries to actively create this state through the repeated use of a mantra, visualization, or other technique. In what I later called Quantum Consciousness, I found that, once experienced, all I had to do was shift my attention to re-enter, and open a space in which this could occur.

My next leap in understanding came when I experienced the observer and that which it created (my thoughts, feelings, sensations, beliefs, etc.) as being the same at a fundamental level. On a superficial level, I had perceived these as different and had given them different names or labels. For example, I had some sensations moving in my body. I labeled these sensations "fear" and decided that *that* (fear) was not good and something I did not want. Hence, I began to resist this energy that "I" had labeled as fear. What "I" realized was that "I" had labeled this energy fear and "I" decided I didn't want it. When I stopped deciding I didn't want the fear, and took off the label and saw it as simply energy, there was no longer a problem. The fear was at its most fundamental level made of energy—hardly something I needed to resist. (More about this in chapter 4.)

Actually, this corresponded greatly to noted physicist David Bohm's idea that there is an "explicate order" and "implicate order." The explicate order is the world as we typically perceive it: full of objects with apparent differences and boundaries. The implicate order is the unbroken wholeness that connects us all; it is the quantum level where objects, and particles, and people, and emotions are made, sub-atomically, of the same substance. On the explicate level, the observer and that which is observed (thoughts, emotions, sensations) appear to be different. On the implicate level, however, they are one and the same. When I was absorbed in this implicate state of interconnection, the line of demarcation between the observed/creator and the observed/created disappeared and I was left in a quiet wholeness.

To explain further, the explicate level is where my thoughts appear to be different from the chair, my arm appears different than your arm. On an implicate level however, there is an underlying unity or quantum level where everything connects with everything else.

Now when I had an experience of sadness, I realized that the observer of the sadness and the sadness itself were fundamentally the same; it was only my perspective of it at an explicate level that split the experience into one of contrast or I-Thou-ness. At the quantum, subatomic level, the composition of what we experience as space and what we experience as physical matter is identical— there is no difference between space (emptiness) and physical matter. In Einstein's words, "Everything is emptiness and form is condensed emptiness." (More about this in Chapter 7.) Sub-atomically, there is no difference between the chair, the sofa, my arm, my pen, my hair follicles, the refrigerator, and the air or empty space in between it all. If you were to look through a "subatomic lens" the world at its most basic level would look like particles floating in emptiness—a pain-free state (or no-state state) from which "my" personal problems would appear and disappear.

One day while contemplating all this, I began to "look for" the being or person or self who had been doing all the meditating, all the witnessing, all the creating, the "me-beyond-observer-created re-alities" who had experienced the observer and the creator as the same. The more "I" looked for who was experiencing this feeling or that thought, who was practicing meditation, the more I saw that there was *no one there*, just empty space. "I" found nothing. That which was doing all those things, and all those things which were being done or created, and the consciousness of "I"—were all the same. There was no separate, individual "I," because "I" cannot exist as a separate entity unless the "I" is fundamentally different from or separate from everything else.

At first, I wasn't able to remain in this "no-state state" for long; I would re-enter the observer-created state as soon as I turned my awareness outward and would resume creating, fusing with, and becoming the experience of my thoughts and feelings. However, the implicate level of unbroken wholeness that I had visited became increasingly easier to re-enter. I would drop into it in times of stress and fatigue as well as when things were going fine. Although I would pop out of it as often as I popped into it, the unity consciousness became an ever-present knowingness or presence that brought a tremendous comfort and peace to whatever endeavor I was engaged in.

The point of having an experience of Quantum Consciousness is to open the doorway into a larger reality that provides a larger context in which to "hold" our experience. Instead of experiencing pain, isolation, frustration, or separateness as absolute states unto themselves, one gains a residing sense of the larger whole, of how, in physicist David Bohm's terminology, "everything is connected to everything else." While the sense of being connected to, even indivisible from, the rest of creation tends to come and go—one does not experience Quantum Consciousness 24 hours a day—the periodic experience of it loosens the hold of previous, limited patterns of thinking and believing. Even a single shift into Quantum Consciousness can change the way you relate to chronic patterns in a lasting way.

Here the Eastern tradition precedes our new Western quantum view of things. Ancient yoga texts call this state in which there is no "I," *samadhi*; Zen Buddhist texts, *satori*. It is also suggested in these writings that as samadhi is experienced more often, the knots or patterns of the mind loosen and have less power.

Why would I want to experience that I and the chair and the sofa and the rest of the universe are the same at the subatomic level?

What will that do for me when I get up in the morning, drink my coffee, and head off to the freeway?

My answer is based primarily on my personal experience. I find that life becomes very even. Any experience of Quantum Consciousness, even when it is not vivid in one's awareness 24 hours a day, begins to take away the judgment, the evaluation, the pain of separation that typically contaminate daily experience. Instead of believing absolutely in the boundaries and appearances of separation, competition, pain, and conflict, another window of consciousness is opened upon an experience of a larger unity.

Quantum Consciousness is essentially unity consciousness—certainly not a new concept in the history of humankind. Eastern traditions (and even some Western philosophies and religions) have been telling us for a very long time that there is an underlying unity that connects us all. The individual could move toward the experience of underlying unity along any number of pathways. In the past, however, you had to take on a belief system in order to follow a particular pathway. In the ancient, traditional pathways, one first had to take on the role of Eric Hoffer's *True Believer* and become a devotee of the master who taught "it"—*it* being enlightenment (or belief in one particular system) and the pathway (or "how to") of achieving it.

What is different about the quantum approach to unity consciousness is the role of science as the herald of it. The role of science in our past shaped a far more limited, one-dimensional universe. The central principle of Newtonian physics, which reduced the world to simple units of *cause* yielding a predictable *effect*, is at the core of contemporary psychology and even Eastern pathways. One set of events in childhood is seen as the cause of certain behaviors in adulthood. A particular technique of meditation is supposed to yield certain, even *predictable* and "*guaranteed*," results.

How often had I personally experienced this see-saw of promised cause/effect formulas, only to be disappointed. Countless times I had been promised that doing "X" (be it spiritual or psychological) would absolutely bring an end to my discomfort. Diligently I would practice the given remedy (be it meditation, or deep-tissue body-work, or acting out the different parts of myself, etc.), only to remain in pain.

The discoveries of quantum physics turned Newton's ordered world upside down. In 1976 when I came across Fritjof Capra's book, *The Tao of Physics*, I read with fascination about a new principle afoot named "non-locality," called by noted physicist Henry Stapp, "the most profound discovery of science." (Stapp, 1977:191) In *Einstein's Moon* physicist F. David Peat described the work of physicist John Stewart Bell, whose theorem (appropriately called "Bell's Theorem") states that there are "no local causes" in the universe. The explanation of Bell's "proof" is complicated, but in essence, it states that the linear cause-effect relationship of Newtonian physics does not exist.

Shock waves rippled through the scientific community in 1964 when Bell first published his findings, and the shock waves continue to this day. The giant called Science, long lulled by the refrain of Newtonian physics, was finally aroused. Turning its die-hard linear gaze (cause/effect) in a non-linear (non-local) direction, it was shaken through and through. The principles of Sir Isaac Newton, which have served as the very foundation of Science (as well as psychology), have rumbled and splintered apart, only to reveal a whole new foundation of interrelationships that leaves some scientists in horror and others in awe. The giant's world is not as we have believed—and what we thought was reality is turning out to be a fairy tale.

Most psychological and spiritual systems require faith and belief. The quantum approach, which arises from a perception of the *relativity of beliefs*, asks one to recognize its validity from subjective experience only. If it does not resonate with you, if it doesn't work for you, forget it. It doesn't mean you aren't ready, aren't pure enough, aren't surrendered enough, aren't evolved enough. It simply means it isn't for you. For sure, it is not for everybody.

In the next chapter we will explore Quantum Consciousness through a series of levels that are the stepping stones of Quantum Psychology. With each level the reader is asked to experiment with exercises that pave the inner way through the increasingly boundless journey of Quantum Psychology.

TWO

THE STEPPING STONES OF QUANTUM CONSCIOUSNESS

Quantum physics has produced a stunning sub-atomic mosaic that demonstrates the underlying unity of the universe—not to the naked eye, perhaps, but within the physical realm. Which means that we have things considerably easier than our predecessors when it comes to probing the "nature of reality." Many challenges still remain, however. It is not easy to bridge the formidable gap between the invisible, sub-atomic level of particles and waves floating in emptiness and the practical, very visible nature of our daily lives. But it is possible.

In attempting to bridge the gap for myself, I began to view the process in terms of "levels of consciousness". Each "level" actually denotes particular understandings and experiences that one might go through in order to "move on" to the next level. This can be likened to "rights of passage," in which with each new experiential understanding of an aspect of consciousness, one becomes freer to move to the next aspect of consciousness, or level of understanding. These passages I call "quantum jumps" through which one passes. As one passes through one aspect of consciousness, new doorways are opened, new experiences explored, and one can move on through the next aspect of consciousness. My tally was seven levels, but there is nothing absolute about the number. It simply reflects the stages or levels I have experienced.

These levels are the "map" of Quantum Consciousness. To quote noted philosopher Alfred Korzybski in *Science and Sanity*, however, *"The map is not the territory."* The point is not to create another map or model to which a group of people adhere, but to provide simple exercises that stimulate new experience in practitioners in such a way that the window through which they view their reality can begin to shift. Each step is comprised of a concept that reflects a specific level of Quantum understanding and a series of exercises though which the concept can be experienced on all levels—mentally, sensorially, emotionally, physically, and spiritually.

Before dipping into the essential characteristics of each level, it is important to appreciate the core principles that differentiate Quantum Psychology from modern psychotherapy ,which is based on what we could call "Newtonian psychology."

Psychotherapy is based on the principles of Newtonian physics, as mentioned in the previous chapter. The gist of these principles is visually captured in the billiard ball metaphor in which the structure and movement of each billiard ball can be clearly defined and predicted. When billiard ball *A* is struck, it will move toward pocket *A*. This is a very orderly world. Isaac Newton, certainly a genius and innovator of his time, described a reductionist view of the world: everything could be reduced down to small units, acting and reacting upon one another, in a cause-and-effect measurable, predictable pattern.

When these principles are translated into psychotherapeutic assumptions, each person is viewed as a separate entity unto itself, who is clearly disconnected from every other person, object, structure, or form, and who goes through the day experiencing a linear series of stimulus-response, cause-and-effect relationships. Unity consciousness is not discussed. Indeed, in *some* schools of psychotherapy, there is no consciousness whatsoever—rather, human functioning is viewed as a complex string of stimulus-response pathways. When consciousness *is* admitted as an operative concept, it is seen as something to be altered, reframed, cured, changed, heightened, or healed. Consciousness is taught to solve problems in itself by identifying cause-and-effect relationships that explain and then hopefully change the problematic dynamic. For example, a client who comes to therapy complaining about his poor relationship with women is suggesting that some relationship with a women, probably his mother, has *caused* the problem.

By contrast, in the quantum approach to consciousness we are interested in providing experiential pathways by which you can begin to perceive and relate to a quantum universe—a universe in which the "facts" of observer-created realities and the inherent interconnectedness of all things are recognized and experienced. While most forms of therapy focus on helping the client to become a "whole" person, Quantum Psychology expands this context of whole personhood to include the rest of the universe. By leading you through a series of levels that slowly unravels the previous limited world view of separation and linear, cause-and-effect relationships, you eventually no longer experience yourself as "separate from" or "a victim of..."

Many schools of psychotherapy focus on integrating "parts" of an individual. For example, let's say that a part of you as a child pretended that things were okay and behaved in a certain way so that your mother would love you. Another part, however, was really angry and always tried to prove Mother was wrong. Conventional psychotherapeutic approaches would encourage the angry child within to express itself, and the pleasing child to give up trying to please Mom. Or the two parts might be "reframed" as survival and growth mechanisms containing resources that can be used in adult life. Perhaps your drive to prove your mother wrong somehow led you to develop successful business skills later on. Still other therapies would contend that if the psycho-emotional state is "owned" as part of the person, then the problem (whatever it is) would be resolved. Most forms of psychotherapy involve some attempt to create a "new" belief over the old problematic one, pre-supposing and judging that it is better to have a "good" program, belief, or decision rather than a "bad" program, belief, or decision.

Quantum approaches to psychotherapy create levels of under-standing that lead one to experience *interconnection* as the context rather than conflicting parts. In the above example, the adult would learn to observe reactions called "Pleasing Child" and "Angry Child" as observer-created realities that were created *in response to* particular experiences with the mother. Ultimately, the goal is to experience the common underlying interconnectedness throughout all responses. Once the larger context is experienced, the specific responses begin to lose their definition and their significance.

It is for these reasons that the quantum approach does not emphasize integrating the false selves of early childhood; it is not concerned with reframing trauma into resource; and it does not reprogram beliefs. Above all, Quantum Psychology is interested in the *you* that is there beyond all the parts, all the traumas, all the false selves. Indeed, the pure experience of Quantum Consciousness is not about integrating anything; it is about *recognizing and experiencing the underlying unity*—the underlying *absence* or interconnection of all parts, so to speak. This underlying experience of unity is where the true wholeness can be experienced and actually is the context for everything. More importantly, this is the context that already is. It is a matter of recognition of that which is, namely, the common unity that we all share. This is the space where problems disappear and *you* emerge. Stated another way, you become the never-changing background and problems, be they psychological or emotional, are seen as an everchanging fore-ground. In a nutshell modern psychology is interested in the foreground, Quantum Psychology is interested in the background. This does not mean a denial of foreground, but ultimately a unity of foreground and background. (More about this in chapters 9 and 10.)

Modern psychotherapy emphasizes a whole or authentic *self*. When the quantum perspective is added, the therapeutic goal is extended beyond integration of the singular self to include a relationship with the larger cosmos. Modern psychotherapy has its roots in problem-resolution, whereas Quantum approaches identify problems as caused by the sense of separation and provide experiences of underlying interconnection.

Now let's dip our toes briefly into the seven different levels before examining their origins and implications in succeeding chapters. Each level represents a "quantum jump" in understanding. *Quantum jump* is a specific term in physics that refers to the nature of change that occurs in particles:

> In place of a continuous change is a discontinuous leap. At one instance the elementary particle is inside the nucleus. At the next it has escaped. There is no intermediate state, no time in which the particle is actually in the process of getting out. Unlike a mouse, a quantum particle will never be discovered with its head poking out and its tail sticking in. Quantum theorists call this discontinuous transition, the quantum jump. (Peat, 1990:15)

> An instant before the jump, the elementary particle is occupying a given region of space. An instant later it is somewhere else and according to the quantum theory no physical process connects these two physical states of being, no duration of time separates them. It is as if the elementary particle suddenly flickered out of existence, passed through a limbo of no time and no space and then reappeared somewhere else. At one instant the particle is inside the nucleus and the next it is travelling around at a high speed. Nothing happens in between. This is the mystery of the quantum jump. (Peat, 1990:19)

In psychological terms, "quantum jump" points to a change that has taken place that cannot be tracked. For example, a person can do different types of therapy for 20 years, looking for the one idea, method, or activity that will free him from a particular emotional block. At some point in time it happens, and there is no way to identify which of the hundred therapeutic variables have "caused" the change. But something happens that we can't identify and the person has moved from one state (emotional block) to another, less limited state (no emotional block).

So it is with each level of understanding that successively "removes" a level of limitation. At some point, perhaps after practicing the exercises that accompany each step or "quantum jump," a change occurs and you find yourself at a new level of consciousness. With each step, the radius of your perception widens to encompass an ever-expanding horizon.

Level 1

As the observer of the contents of my mind (thoughts, feeling, emotions, sensations, associations), I am more than the contents of my mind.

Anyone who has studied Eastern traditions will recognize the obvious origins of this first level. The cornerstone of most meditation disciplines is the practice of observing, "witnessing," or being mindful of the contents of one's mind or state-of-being. Thus one observes specific thoughts, images, sensations, feelings, and emotions as they occur and, in the process, gains a sense of being separate from or more than the flow of these contents.

Once an observer begins to appreciate that he is *not* his thoughts, feelings, and emotions, but rather an observing presence, a process of disidentification is inaugurated that gradually constellates as the first bridge to Quantum Consciousness.

Level 2

Everything (thoughts, feelings, emotions, sensations, associations) is made of energy.

Here we approach the first aspect of the work of noted physicist Dr. David Bohm. Bohm says that the world is made of energy, space, mass, and time. At Level 2 we look at our relationship with energy.

Once you have experienced yourself as the observer, then you can begin to experience how all the things you observe going on in "your mind" are made of the same underlying energy. Anger is made of the same energy that joy is. Level 2 allows you to remove the labels or content that typically categorize various facets of experience as being different, thus automatically diffusing or neutralizing the charge of whatever experience you are observing.

Level 3

I am the creator of what I observe.

This section looks at the work of physicist Dr. Werner Heisenberg and his *Uncertainty Principle*. Heisenberg demonstrated that the observer creates that which he/she observes. In Quantum Psychology terminology: we create our *subjective* experience. Although this will be elaborated on in great detail in Chapter 5, to summarize it here, this level also takes us through David Bohm's "mass" aspect as an ingredient of the universe along with, its *part*-(icle) nature.

In the Eastern tradition emphasis is placed solely on the person doing the witnessing. There is no mention of any causal relationship between the thoughts that are observed and the person doing the observing. The implication is that the two phenomena—thought and observer-of-thought—are quite separate in essence.

Quantum physics introduced me to my next bridging concept via the principle of "observer-created reality," which states: (1) There is no reality in the absence of observation and, (2) observation creates reality (Herbert, 1985). Put simply, you as the observer create the subjective reality you are observing.

The importance of Level 3 in pragmatic terms is that it empowers you beyond the passive position of witness to the active position of creator. Once you understand, for example, that you create your own sadness, or depression, or anxiety, you can stop creating it. This bridge leads us further out of the dense forest of Newtonian thought toward the ranging freedom of Quantum Consciousness.

Level 4 *and* Level 5

The physical universe is made of Energy, Space, Mass and Time

At Level 2 we experienced that whatever we observe in ourselves—thoughts, emotions, sensations, etc.—is all made of energy. At Level 3 we recognized that we are the creators of what we experience, and the mass aspect of the physical universe. Now at Level 4 we learn more about the time aspect of our universe and how time is a concept created by us. At Level 5, we move through the most unnoticed aspect of our world: the space that is ever present. At this level we come in contact with the changeless nature of space, and explore how by touching it our experience is transformed.

As was mentioned previously, David Bohm discovered that the physical universe is an "unfolding" and "enfolding" of four main elements: energy, space, mass, and time (duration). Everything that exists in the world as we know it—from the subtle titillation of a loving feeling to the construction of a concrete wall—has these four primary elements. Thus the underlying energy we experience at Level 2 can now be more precisely described as the unfolding and enfolding of energy, space, mass, and time.

Perceiving this expansion was an important bridge for me. If I found myself in an observer-created reality of anger, it somehow helped me enormously to experience the implicate commonality between myself—what I created (anger), and the object of my anger (another person). By contemplating the common ingredients of energy, mass, space, time, I gained a kind of *textural comprehension* of the underlying unity. It became easier to experience the illusory nature of the boundaries I was creating and temporarily believing in, once I realized that my creation (i.e., anger) is comprised of energy, space, mass, and time: the observer/creator (me) is made of energy, space, mass, and time, and the person who is the object of my anger is made of energy, space, mass, and time. In other words, we as creators, that which we create, and the recipient or object of our creation are all made of the same substance.

Stated in Quantum Psychology terminology, in order for a problem such as an unwanted emotion to exist, it must possess energy, occupy a space, have measurable mass (solidity), and exist in time (have duration—a beginning, middle, and an end). Examining a problem in terms of these four parameters can provide a far more multi-dimensional framework than the current, binary system of traditional therapeutic models in which problems are viewed in a linear cause/effect relationship.

Level 4 and Level 5 take you into a new realm of primal essence and provide exercises that prepare you to tap into the freedom of experiencing yourself and your world on a boundless, quantum level.

Level 6

"Everything interpenetrates everything else."
Dr. David Bohm

In practical terms, this level removes the iron-curtain divisions that we typically take for granted. We assume for example, that the feelings of "I like myself" and "I hate myself" are fundamentally, irrevocably *different*—that success is obviously separate from failure. The world as we know it is overflowing with boundaries that demarcate the differences.

At Level 6 we travel through the intoxicating world of David Bohm's explicate and implicate orders, where what is manifest and what is invisible are continuously "enfolding" and "unfolding", where all boundaries are observer-created rather than inherent. This is the quantum bridge that takes us beyond judgments and evaluations and introduces us to the experience of underlying unity. The sixties' injunction to "go with the flow" is genuinely possible with the experience of this level. As your Quantum Consciousness of this level deepens, you will begin to experience the world far beyond the confines of observer-created realities.

Level 7

"Everything is made of emptiness and form is condensed emptiness." (Einstein) In other words, everything is made of the same substance.

Albert Einstein's quotation about the relationship between form and emptiness bears a striking resemblance to a Buddhist principle stated over 2,500 years ago in *The Heart Sutra*: "Form is none other than emptiness and emptiness is none other than form." Both quotations, one from a rich and ancient spiritual tradition, one the product of 20th-century science, make the same statement about the nature of the universe: everything in it, including the space in which everything exists, is all made of the same substance or emptiness. And; physical and non-physical reality are the same.

Everything in the physical universe has *form*; form creates what Bohm called the *explicate order* of sizes, shapes, mass, density— from air to leaves to couches to people. If we looked through a "sub-atomic lens" at a couch or leaf, however, we would see particles/waves floating in what looks like nothing—what we would call emptiness, a void. It would be like looking at a black sky on a starlit night. The stars are the form; the sky is the emptiness. From a quantum perspective, the fascinating point is that the emptiness that surrounds the stars *and* the stars themselves are both made of the same material. When I look at the sky, I see what looks like very different substances—solid particles we call "stars", open empty space we call "sky—but it's really nice to know that on another level it's all the same substance.

In order for there to be a "you" and a "me," there has to be consensual boundaries that create the appearance of a distinction between you and me, between chairs and tables, between trees and sky. These consensual boundaries constitute how we normally perceive the world, how we live at the explicate level of form. When we get some sense that these boundaries do not exist on the quantum level—that what we perceive as wide-open space is composed of the same particles and waves as objects we perceive as dense and "physical"—then the limited, isolating experience of *you-ness* and *me-ness* dissolves into a comforting space of union and knowingness.

At Level 6 we experience the interconnection of all things. Level 7 takes us one step further by saying that not only does everything overlap, but everything is actually made of the same material. The relationship between objects thus moves beyond one of interpenetration to a level of universal sameness or oneness. It's more than saying, "Edward's energy overlaps Lucy's energy"; it's saying that the substance that comprises the body we call "Edward" is identical to that which we call "Lucy." There isn't just overlap—on the quantum level there is pure, unbroken "is-ness."

This book could not be written in the quantum consciousness of Level 7 because it is impossible, at this level of "perception" or "knowingness," to make the distinctions required for description and exposition. The joke is that by the time you are actually able to experience Level 7, this book no longer exists as a separate object with distinguishing characteristics. Or perhaps it is more realistic to say that just as you recognized the true lack of boundaries between yourself and the world around you, you would also recognize the non-quantum nature of this book that, ironically, is all about Quantum Consciousness. As one of the founders of quantum physics, Neils Bohr, stated, "There is no such thing as a quantum world, just a quantum description" (Herbert, 1985).

Now we are back to that annoying question of my friend, "Why would I want to disappear into the soup of everything else?" Given that religious and philosophical traditions across the centuries have proffered basic ideas of Level 7 as the highest achievement of human consciousness, there must be something appealing in it.

To experience the "end point" of Quantum Consciousness is to experience the fundamental freedom from separated, individual selfhood. To arrive at the experience requires us, paradoxically, to interact with our selfhood in some way. Eastern traditions have erected thousands of monasteries and temples to provide structure and location for how that interaction is to take place. The purpose of the quantum approach is to provide a way for recognizing unity consciousness that is both experiential and practical, a way that enables people to develop a new context in which problem resolution can occur more easily.

Finding the useful, life-enhancing applications of Level 7—as well as exploring its further reaches—will be the subject of Chapter

9. For now, it is enough to hold an open mind to the possibility that there is an experience of expansion to be found in this culminating Level of Quantum Consciousness.

THREE

GETTING OUT OF THE THICK OF THINGS

I'm just sittin here watching the wheels go round and round...I really love to watch them roll...no longer ridin on the merry-go-round...I just had to let it go...I just had to let it go...I just had to let it go.

John Lennon

The "Me Generation" of the past two decades has taken us into a psychological land of deep attachments and fierce identifications. Our culture of narcissism, as some have termed these times, encourages us to name our wants, desires, and wishes and "go for it." In order to rev up the steam required to "go for it," however, we first have to invest a great amount of ourselves in ideals, objects, and values that lie outside us. This means we have to *identify* with them—strongly—or we wouldn't be willing to exert effort to get them.

From a quantum perspective, there is nothing "wrong" with attachments and identifications; they are simply a sliver of the total pie of human consciousness. From the point of view of personal experience, however, attachments and identifications generally lead to discomfort, dissatisfaction, and even pain. When performing some aspect of your job poorly (as everyone is bound to do at least once in a lifetime) results in feeling humiliated, stupid, incompetent, or just plain depressed, then you are identifying with your job in a way that causes pain. If you feel overwhelmed by feelings of inadequacy each time a task, event, or interaction doesn't go your way, it is because you are, in essence, looking at yourself through a peashooter. The result is a very confined and limited sense of self that is also usually quite fragile.

Quantum physics has made it possible for us to put away our peashooters once and for all, and don, instead, what I call a "quantum lens." Looking at life through this quantum lens offers a vastly more expansive vista than we are accustomed to beholding. It also alters the very boundaries upon which our current world is based. Like stepping into a transporter room on Star Trek's *Enterprise* and suddenly dematerializing there only to reconstellate someplace else, the quantum lens also acts as a transporter—so that what was once a clearly defined object or body with a great deal of mass and weight now becomes a shimmering pattern of particles capable of transcending the space/time barrier.

But first things first. Before we experience the more breathtaking aspects of Quantum Consciousness, some basic pathways have to be established in order for us to exchange our peashooters for quantum lenses.

Learning to Observe the Invisible

Level I: The "Wave" Function

As the observer of the contents of my mind (thoughts,
feelings, emotions, sensations, associations), I am more
than the contents of my mind.

Before you can do anything about how you feel, you have to be
able to observe or witness it. The moment you attempt to see what's
going on inside of you, part of you separates off to make this
observation. In philosophical terms, it's called "self-reflection"; in
psychosynthesis terms, it's called "disidentification." G. I. Gurdjieff
called it "self-observation," the Hindus and Buddhists called it
"witnessing" and the Zen Buddhists, "mindfulness". In the last 25
years it has not been uncommon in psychotherapy circles, like
Gestalt, to ask a client to "be aware" of a pattern. In Hakomi therapy
recently developed by Ron Kurtz, mindfulness is emphasized.
Certainly, whether we called it awareness, mindfulness, observation, or witnessing, disciplines of the East, West, and Middle East
have employed it in some way to help the individual enhance
personal freedom.

Whatever the name, the essence is *observation*. Thus the
purpose of this first quantum level is to teach you how to *observe*
your internal experience rather than fusing with it and being
consumed by it.

This observation gives you an experience of looking at your life
events without judgment, evaluation, significance or preference.
For most of us, judgments, likes, and dislikes pop up automatically,
so that we "find ourselves" disliking a person, or we "find ourselves" loathing a particular event. Rather than consciously choosing
a response, reactions *happen to us*, often beyond our control. These
automatic reactions greatly color and shape how we perceive and
experience the world around us, and as long as the reactions remain
on "automatic," we remain unable to choose how we feel, how we
live.

The moment you use part of your awareness to observe a
reaction, in essence you are putting a distance between you and the

response. In that space, you are not consumed by the reaction. Even as the reaction runs its course, the space of observation creates a distance that diminishes your sense of attachment to it.

Because Quantum Consciousness is an *experience* more than it is a concept, it is useful to create an environment in which to experience this response/reaction phenomenon. In this spirit, Quantum exercises and contemplations (which can be practiced alone, in pairs, or in small groups) accompany each quantum Level.

Quantum Exercise 1

• •

Sit comfortably and let your eyes close gently. Intentionally recall an incident that upset you. It might or might not involve other people. It could be the toilet overflowing while you're home alone, or it could involve an angry, nonverbal exchange with a motorist, a misunderstanding with a clerk, or a clash with a loved one.

Visualize the incident, seeing yourself in the middle of it. *Be* in the middle of it, recreating the scene with all the turmoil and annoyance with which you originally experienced it.

Next, continue to see the very same scene, but also notice that you are watching it. Now there is a you in the scene, experiencing all the emotions and upset, and there is a you outside the scene, in the experience of observation, noticing all the emotions, thoughts, and sensations.

Notice if there is any difference between how you experience the two visualizations.

• •

You might not experience the feeling of objectivity and no preference in the beginning. Most of us are very attached to our responses to things. If we feel we have been insulted, misunderstood, or belittled, we are not usually willing to step outside our righteous emotions too quickly. If you find yourself unable to move to the second visualization, stay with the first part, being in the middle of it, until some of the charge of the event is drained off. Eventually, you will begin to feel willing to let part of your awareness move into the neutrality of observation.

You can also imagine yourself inside an empty theater with a large screen, on which you project your visualization of the upsetting experience. The you sitting in the theater chair observes the you in the middle of the experience. As you watch your own "movie," ideally you become less fused with the story. If the story remains upsetting—for example, you are picturing yourself as a "bad" mother losing your temper with your child—then intentionally allow yourself to feel the "bad mother" feelings. Do this intensely for a minute, then release the visualization, relax for a few minutes, and then create it again. Each and every human being is drawn back to experience those events, feelings, and traumas that were resisted initially. Most of us resist feeling bad, in general. Sometimes, the need to experience something is so great, that it is not possible to move to the observation mode without first allowing yourself to be submerged in whatever has been resisted.

However, the moment you *intentionally* allow yourself to experience a resisted emotion or event, no matter how submerged you may feel in it, the very fact that you consciously chose to experience it creates the pathway to the freeing, neutral space of observation.* As you shift in and out of submerging yourself in the experience and then observing yourself in the experience, you begin to actually sense the *you* that is present for both levels. As you recall the emotional experience, realize that prior to it you were there and that after its affects had fully spent themselves you were still there. The You, or observer of your experience, is always there; it notices all the thoughts, sensations, and feelings that come and go.

I had one client who described the difference between being completely submerged in the experience versus having part of herself in the observation space as "having more room to breathe:"

---

* Although this is not the time to delve deeply into another realm of physics called "chaos theory," it is important to note that what most of us resist more than anything in our lives is *chaos*. You can give chaos other names—feeling overwhelmed, anxiety, confusion, being out of control, feeling crazy—but its essence is resisted experience. This resisted experience causes the formation of chronic identity patterns. The relationship between chaos theory and resisted experience is discussed in detail in my forthcoming book, *The Tao of Chaos: Quantum Consciousness Vol. 2.*

"When I'm all wrapped up in the experience, there is a feeling of contraction and narrowness—kind of like I'm trapped in long corridors with no windows and no doors. Once I move part of myself into observation, there's more room to move—the corridors widen immediately, and I get a feeling of space, of air, even of light coming in."

Observation leads to an experience of the self as being *more than* the thoughts, feelings, emotions, and sensations that frequently buffet it. If we remain tightly identified with the comings and going of the mind, there is no room for experiencing things in any other way. We are, in essence, captives of a very narrow, entrenched set of beliefs and viewpoints. Learning to observe opens our psychological windows, letting in the light and air of expanded perspectives.

The experience of Level 1 is the experience of being *more than* what troubles you. If a part of you can witness or observe your feeling of sadness over the breakup of a relationship, then that means that you are not *just* your sadness—just as you are not the picture you draw to image your sadness. There is the feeling of sadness—perhaps there is the picture of sadness—and behind or beyond both is the *you* that observes these different facets of experience we call sadness.

Consider the same event from two different modes of experiencing it. The scenario is: I have turned in a monthly report to my boss, which he usually approves and compliments. This time I am called into his office, the door is shut, and he impatiently tells me there is a major oversight in my report, which will have to be completely redone. I flush in surprise and embarrassment, my palms sprout beads of perspiration, and my stomach feels like it was hit with a two-by-four. I mutter my apologies and return to my embarrassment breaking over me. My breathing is shallow, my heart is beating rapidly, and all I want to do is run out of the building. I feel stupid, I feel grossly inadequate, and I also feel enraged.

If I choose to practice the quantum principle of Level 1, I will have a very different experience of the same event. Anything I can witness, I can go beyond. Philosopher Alfred Korsybski stated it as "anything you know about cannot be you." If I can begin to observe and witness my reactions, than I will feel freer and more at peace.

It is only by the identification and fusion with a thought or feeling that I limit myself from being the observer to becoming the experience itself. In my previous book, *Trances People Live : Healing Approaches in Quantum Psychology*, I describe this as the process of going into trance, "the fusion and merging with thoughts, feelings, emotions, and past associations."

In the above experience, if I totally identify with the feelings of humiliation and embarrassment, and if I couple this psycho-emotional process with the decision that "this is me," then I am confined to the parameters and boundaries of the experience labeled "humiliation and embarrassment." However, if I shift part of my attention to the level of observation, then other options become available. If I can observe my reactions, then I can go beyond them. I can step out of "my" reactions and begin to notice them. Then I can begin to choose, observe, notice the pattern, and so on. As I comprehend, even for a moment, that I exist outside of my thoughts and emotions, they have less effect on me.

This truth became profoundly real for me in June of 1980 in India. At about 6 o'clock in the morning as I was walking to a bus station, my mind was holding its usual banter of conversation. Suddenly I experienced myself outside of, or larger than, or beyond what I was thinking or feeling.

What was more astounding was that an observing "I," which was me was always there. The smaller I's of "i feel good" or "i feel bad," or "i love myself" or "i hate my self," were transient. The observing "I" was always present. I realized at that time, that no wonder "I" felt so insecure. I was identifying with an "i" that came and went, rather than the observing I, or witnessing presence. I asked myself, who has witnessed all my thoughts, feelings, and happenings of "my" life? I laughed as I realized "I" was the witness. I asked myself who came first, me the observing "I," or the emotional upset that had been bothering me. Again, obviously, the same observing "I" was there before, during, and after the upset. My experience of myself was permanently transformed as I laughed at myself for missing what was so obvious—*me*—the observing "I" that was always there watching all the transient i's.

The realness of that new consciousness never left me and continued to solidify and deepen for me on an experiential level— the first level of Quantum Psychology.

Is It Dissociation or
Is It Observation?

When you learn to observe, you learn to separate, dis-associate, or dis-identify yourself from what you are observing. Even if you are noticing what is being experienced—there has to be a little distance, just to notice or be aware of. Does this mean you go into denial? Into dissociation? Is "space" the same as amnesia? Although meditation is intended for dis-association, it can be used as a way of "spiritualizing dissociation." Since the approaches in Level 1 originate in Eastern meditation methods, I think it is important to discuss this issue.

With our society's new awareness of the psychology of abuse, we are also quite concerned with what is called "dissociation" in clinical circles. Dissociation is an automatic defense that protects you during trauma. Dissociation occurs when you split off from an experience, refusing to feel the pain or fear or humiliation of a painful event. Usually, we learn to dissociate as children, when we have few internal defenses to fall back upon. A child who is molested by her father cannot allow herself to fully feel the horror, so she "shuts down" part of her reaction by splitting off from it. In its most severe form, dissociation results in Multiple Personality Disorder, something most of us know about only through movies such as *Sybil*.

The two main characteristics of dissociation are that it occurs *automatically*, and that it allows a person to *not experience* something. When a child dissociates from feelings of abandonment, for example, the split-off from feeling occurs automatically and unconsciously, as a way of protecting the child. This closing over an unbearable emotional wound is just like skin cells automatically beginning to generate over a physical wound without any conscious thought on the part of the injured person.

The dis-association of self-observation, by contrast, allows you to become aware of *what you are already feeling*, and happens only as a consequence of *conscious choice*. As I begin to feel anxious, I can consciously choose to use part of my awareness to observe what I am feeling, rather than sinking into the quicksand of anxious feelings as though it were the only available internal landscape. The attitude behind the observing or witnessing activity is not one of, "I shouldn't have this feeling," or "I hope this passes quickly." *Observation is free of judgments, evaluation, significance and preference.* When you are in true observation, you feel *free to experience* the emotion and *free to stop experiencing it.* By contrast, dissociation is a process that leaves you free only *not* to experience the emotion; you are not free to experience it, as the way you are when observing. *Dis-association* in observation runs equally in all directions of experience: you are free to feel sad, anxious, happy, and you are equally free to choose to not feel the particular effect.

Meditation and observation practices, however, can certainly be misused as a way of attempting to dissociate from uncomfortable or threatening feelings. And it is certainly true that many abused people have found solace in meditation, because the *disidentification* that is the goal of many Eastern approaches seems so similar to the patterns of *dissociation* underlying their own emotional lives.

The differences between dissociation and Quantum observation are crucial, *Dissociation is born of trauma*, it happens automatically and unconsciously as a survival tactic, and it anesthetizes feelings and emotions. *Quantum observation is born of choice*, it is chosen consciously and intentionally and encompasses whatever is being felt and thought. The space that occurs as a result of observing an ongoing experience is not a space of denial, or amnesia, or blankness. It is actually the space of *allowance* whereby *nothing need be excluded from awareness.*

Let me give another example. In the monastery I lived in in India, and certainly in some other spiritual communities, many emotions and thoughts are considered "impure," "bad," a "barrier" to enlightenment, etc. Certainly, also in psychotherapy circles there is often an implicit message that anger is something to "work on" and a problem, while "love" is okay and a goal. Often, particularly in the former case, meditation or some transcendent technique is used to repress, or nullify feelings labeled as "bad." In psychology circles, certain techniques reinforce this bad (anger)/ good (love) dichotomy. As will be discussed in detail in Chapter 5, to *prefer* or be *unwilling* to have a particular experience requires a *judgment*. This is not Quantum observation.

The point is not to block an experience of, say, feeling unworthy, but to add to it the state of observing. When you dissociate, you are simply catapulted outside of the conscious arena of feeling—but the feeling remains in a repressed form. In Quantum observation, the feeling is "free to be," but your awareness of it accompanies you through the experience.

Let me state it another way since this a question that comes up in many of my workshops. If you are in Quantum observation you are intentionally dis-associating from (not associating with) a feeling but simultaneously you are *free to feel* the feeling and *free not to* feel the feeling. Stated another way, you can have the feeling or not have the feeling. This is Quantum observation. On the other hand, if you can only *not* have the feeling, if you are trying to get away from it or not experience it, and you label it bad, not constructive, or unspiritual, you are dissociating.

A pictorial example might be helpful. A trainee of mine once asked me "How do I know if I am observing and the anger is handled." I picked up my coffee cup by the handle and said, "If I can pick up the coffee cup and put it down it is handled, I am in Quantum observation, and I am free. If I cannot pick-up the anger and put it down, then I am not free. If I cannot pick-up the anger and experience it, then I am *dissociating*."

Some of us are natural *dissociators* and some of us are natural *mergers*. Where you fall on the emotional continuum will affect how you experience the exercises in Level 1. A person who chronically dissociates is going to have a very different time with these exercises than a person who tends to be very emotional. The dissociator will be accustomed to separating himself from his internal responses, whereas the feeler will be accustomed to identifying strongly with each and every response and reaction. If you are a dissociator, learning to observe will seem familiar, but allowing yourself to feel what you're experiencing will be more foreign. If you are a feeler, learning to detach part of yourself in order to observe (rather then respond) will be more foreign. Simply be aware of the aspects of the process that are unfamiliar to you, and observe your responses to the new experience.

If you are unsure which way of functioning is most characteristic for you, think of an experience that disturbs you in any way and then ask yourself two simple questions:

(1) *Am I willing to merge with the experience?*

> If you are dissociating even somewhat, you will not be willing or able to totally merge with the experience of, say, anger, and your answer would be "No." If you tend to respond reactively, your answer would probably be "Yes."

(2) *Am I willing to **not** merge with the experience?*

> Your answer here would be "Yes," if you tend to dissociate from your feelings. By contrast, if you tend to over-identify with your emotional states, your answer would be "No."

If you feel compelled to be angry in a particular situation, then you are not free. Similarly, if you cannot tolerate the feeling of anger, you are not free. Again, imagine a coffee cup in your hand: the freedom to handle it means being free to pick it up and put it down when you choose. Needless to say, dealing with human emotions is far more complicated than picking up and putting down a cup. On an emotional level, this process occurs along a continuum. At first, only two percent of people might be willing to feel the anger, or, for mergers, only two percent of people might be unwilling to feel the anger and observe. The exercises of Level 1 are meant to define a pathway of movement for you along this continuum of being free to experience or to *not* experience a feeling, thought, or emotion.

If you are unwilling to experience a feeling, thought, or emotion, then you can never truly dis-associate from it. You must be willing to *experience* and *not experience* something in order to move into a genuine space of witnessing or observing.

If you find that you are unwilling to experience a particular thought or feeling, intentionally create your resistance to the experience again and again. *Consciously* be unwilling to feel it. In *Trances People Live, Healing Approaches in Quantum Psychology*, I discussed a basic psychodynamic principle that anything you intentionally create in present time (such as resistance to a particular experience), you gain power over. In the case of resistance, consciously choosing to experience it automatically depotentiates it. Paradoxically, *allowing yourself to resist eventually dissolves the resistance*. This way of working is elaborated in Chapter 5, "Getting Back to Zero."

Where Do Feelings Fit In?

When we do not accept our feelings and either repress them into oblivion or judge them as bad, we are creating separation and boundaries within our personal "system." Actually judgement of others or of self is a way we resist experiencing emotions. To process through judgement simply ask yourself; "By being judgemental what experience am I resisting?" What pops-up may give you the emotion that needs to be observed. These judgements create divisions and boundaries within individuals which become the foundation for global division and even war. From a quantum perspective, when you allow yourself to experience the whole feeling, or the whole event, then the sense of division disappears. The basic quantum discovery that "everything is connected to everything else" would seem less foreign to us, less "far out," if there were not so much division and separation *within* us. The point in the quantum perspective is not to separate yourself from your emotions and feelings via denial or dissociation, but to observe and acknowledge them, experience them fully as you observe, and notice their shapes and boundaries in your mind's eye.

How to work more directly with emotions is discussed in detail in the next chapter.

Most of us are fused or identified with one or more past traumatic experiences, even if we don't remember what they are. Once you start observing the contents of your mind, however, you will begin to see your prejudices, your defense mechanisms, your wounds—all the parts that you've disallowed and separated from. Learning to observe the spots of trauma within is the first step toward healing; it is the first "peace offering" from the wounded person to the split-off trauma that has been banished from consciousness for so long.

An Indian teacher, Meher Baba, used a wonderful metaphor to describe this process; "The ego is like an iceberg. Ninety percent of it is underwater. As we observe it, the submerged begins to move into the light of observation, and melts in the light of awareness."

Many years ago I was meditating in my usual way in India. As I observed my thoughts come and go, I noted a familiar one that sounded just like my mother. The thought said, "It's an uphill battle all the way." Normally, I would have automatically merged with that thought and experienced the frustration and futility of its message. This time, however, I was able to observe it and *not identify* with it. For the first time, I felt free of the thought and experienced the open space left by not merging with it.

What Goes Up Must Come Down

This first Level can be extremely powerful in helping you to loosen your sense of identification with each and every experience that comes your way. Whatever you identify with, you are subject to its effects. In more colloquial terms, what goes up must come down. As you notice that thoughts come and go, emotions come and go, sensations come and go, you realize that there is one common factor weaving throughout this huge mosaic of experience: *You*, the observer of all the comings and goings. Once you, as the observer, begin to appreciate that you are not your thoughts, feelings, and emotions, but rather a witnessing presence, a greater clarity emerges.

Noted Sufi Master G. I. Gurdjieff said,

A thing cannot observe itself. A thing identical with itself cannot see itself, because it is the same as itself, and a thing which is the same as itself cannot possibly have a standpoint apart from itself, from which to observe itself (Nicoll, 1984:59).

What Gurdfieff is pointing to is that since you can be aware of and observe a thought or feeling, you must be apart from the thought or feeling. If you were identical to the thoughts or feelings, you couldn't observe them, or even know about them. *Observation and knowing about something suggests a separation*, between it and you.

Some call this presence the inner self, the essence, the "being."

Quantum Exercise 2

● ●

To get a sense of thoughts as things that come and go, very gently let your eyes close as you sit or lie comfort-

ably. Each time a thought crosses your mind, notice it and ask yourself, "To where does this thought subside?"

As you notice the activity in your mind, it appears at first as a pattern of *thought...thought...thought.*

Illustration 1

For example, notice that your mind might throw-up thoughts like "I like my job," "I hate my job," "I love my relationship," I hate my relationship," I'm bored," "I'm excited," "I'm tired." To you it appears like this:

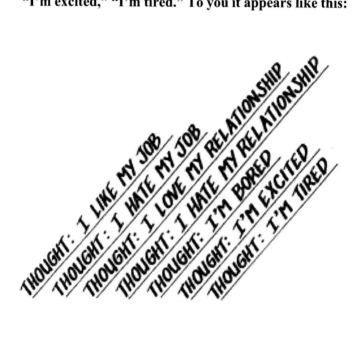

In reality, however, a thought arises and subsides, after which there is a momentary *space* before the next thought arises and subsides.

Illustration 2

Below, we ask the question, "Where does that thought subside. Notice, that there is a space where the thought subsides, before the next thought arises. Stay in the space between two thoughts.

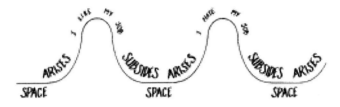

The space between the two thoughts can be seen as Bohm's implicate order, while the thoughts themselves can be seen as Bohm's explicate order. We ask ourselves the question, "To where does that thought subside?" since we are looking for the underlying unity. Tarthang Tulku, noted Buddhist teacher, says it this way:

"As you observe your thoughts passing, watch very sensitively for the moment, when one thought fades and another arises. This transition is very quick and subtle, but involves the momentary availability of a space which you can contact and expand. This space has a quality of openness, free from the usual discursive and discriminative thinking. (Tulku, 1977:58)

● ●

The wave-like image in the illustration calls to mind one of the pivotal questions that plagued quantum physics in the 1920s: Is matter (electrons) made of particles or waves? It seemed made of both. In 1924 physicist de Broglie proposed a revolutionary conception: that electrons possessed a dual nature; that they could be *both* a wave and particle. In this illustration, the *process* of thoughts as they arise and subside appears in wave-like form, but it should also be noted that when you merge with a particular thought or emotion, it becomes more *part*-(icle)-like. In the tradition of Yoga, Patangali's

Yoga Sutras describe thoughts as waves:

> "Patangali defines thought as a wave (vritti) in the mind. Ordinarily a thought-wave arises, remains in the mind for a moment, and then subsides, to be succeeded by another wave." (Isherwood, 1953:121-122)

Throughout this book, I am marking off the word *part*-(icle) like this because often in psychotherapy circles, people say, "There's a *part* of myself which ..." As will be discussed more thoroughly in chapter 4 and chapter 5, a part is separate from the underlying whole. Here, *part*-(icles) are parts, that without a quantum lens seem separate from the whole. Since, as Bohm states, "all parts are connected to the whole," I will use *part*-(icle) to denote psychology's "*part*." By identifying something apart from the whole it becomes more solid, more defined, more fixed or more like a part, with boundaries that separate it from the whole.

Since recent research in quantum physics informs us that matter, energy, space, and time are all fundamentally the same, then they can be viewed as waves, as particles, or as both. In *The Philosphers' Stone*, F. David Peat wrote:

> "The only conceivable conclusion was that electrons have a dual schizophrenic existence. Design an experiment that looks for particle-like behavior, and the electron behaves like a particle. Design one that looks like a wave, and it behaves like a wave." (Peat, 1991:12)

Clearly, the observer creates the outcome—be it particle or wave. For the purposes of this section, thoughts and emotions can be viewed in their wave-like form. In Chapter 5, we will examine them in their *part*-(icle)-like form.

We can ride a thought like a surfer rides a wave and it will take us back into the space between two thoughts—the implicate order. Notice that the space never changes, just as the implicate order never changes. Experiencing this *space between two thoughts* is another way you can begin to feel, sense, experience the comfort and permanence of the underlying quantum unity even as you become accustomed to observing, rather than completely identifying with, the contents of your mind.

The question in this exercise also requires you to make a

division between subject and object in order to answer it. You have to separate from a thought in order to watch it and notice where it ends or subsides and another thought begins. This separation automatically lessens your identification with the thought. Why is it valuable to separate the subject from the object? Why is it valuable to learn how to observe? Because anything you identify with will limit you.

Certainly there are many things you don't mind being limited by: your preference for certain types of women or men is something you enjoy, and you don't experience it as a limitation. Many identifications, however, will cause some discomfort. For one thing, since the nature of the mind is one of continual fluctuation (it is the nature of the mind to change its mind!), the object of your identifications can change so fast you end up lamenting, "I don't know what I want!" One minute you like your job, the next minute you don't. One week you are satisfied with your relationship, the next you feel restless and discontent. If you fall madly in love today, you know that within the month, you will feel differently. The fluctuations we experience in our thinking, feeling, in our physical sensations, in our emotional responses are sometimes dizzying in magnitude. The one source of constancy, bringing a sense of equilibrium and continuity, can be this observer, this witnessing presence, that is always there.

One thought common to every living person at some point in life is "I'm afraid." To be consumed by the thought/feeling "I'm afraid" means to identify with it, to say, "Yep, that's me—*I'm* afraid." Usually, one fearful thought leads to a train of fearful thoughts:

"I'm afraid I'll lose my job."
"I'm afraid I won't have enough money."
"I'm afraid I'll get cancer."
"I'm afraid s/he'll leave me and I'll be all alone."

As you observe the first thought arise, "I'm afraid I'll lose my job," and ask yourself the question, "To where does that thought subside?", you'll probably find that the beginnings of your own personal story begin to pop into your thoughts.

"I've never been able to hold onto a job... not even as a teenager doing trivial part-time work...my father always said I had no perseverance."

Once the thread of the storyline is clear, realize that, in essence, you've said to yourself, "That's me—I have no perseverance—that's just how I am."

The only thing that gives a thought power to affect you in any way is the fact that you have identified with it. Thinking "I have green skin" won't affect you because it is so blatantly not you, there is nothing to hook into. By contrast, thinking "I have no perseverance" has a hook for you in your previous experience. As a psychological process, identification is like glue in that, when you use it, things (thoughts, emotions, sensations) stick to you.

In a workshop, one student commented after doing the exercise, "There was so much space that words didn't make a lot of sense. And before I could ask about the thought it was gone and there was space. It's weird because I couldn't remember the thought, only the space." Another trainee commented at a workshop, "Things don't seem to have the same weight anymore."

In practicing the exercise of Level 1, you create the possibility of having a new experience of non-identification, a glue-free moment of emptiness or openness, a point of experiential silence. Experiencing the emptiness from which everything arises and to which everything subsides is the beginning of Quantum Consciousness.

Quantum Exercise 3

• •

Separating the observer from the observed.

From where does that thought arise?

When a thought arises, ask "From where does that thought arise?

When we continually ask ourselves, "From where does that thought arise?" we soon learn that a thought arises, and subsides, and then there is a space, after each thought.

• •

This Quantum exercise is similar to the previous one, "To where does this thought subside." In the last exercise we are asked to find the empty-space after the arising of a thought. In this exercise we are asked to notice the empty-space (implicate) *prior* to the arising of a thought. One workshop participant asked me, "Why so many similar exercises since all you really need is one." I replied, "Not every exercise will work for you or anyone else. If I offer a menu, you can pick and choose the ones that work and discard the rest." Jokingly I said, "Today's special is to where does this thought subside, it's garnished with the witness, and smothered in the implicate order."

Many years ago, I was working with Nisargadatta Maharaj, an Indian teacher. He asked a woman who was audio taping for a new book, "What will be the name of my next book." She replied, "*Beyond Consciousness.*" He said, "No, *Prior* to Consciousness. Find out who you are *prior* to your last thought and stay there."

"From where does that thought arise?" brings us back to that space so that we can witness the rising and subsiding of each thought.

A common experience is to wake up in the morning; a thought comes by your awareness called "I feel good," and the witness says, "That's me." Your mind will then start coming up with reasons why you feel good: "I feel good because I got a lot of sleep; I feel good because I didn't sleep very much; I feel good because I meditated this morning; because I had a lot for dinner; because I didn't have a lot of dinner." Around noon a thought will come by which says, "I'm tired," and you'll respond, "That's me." "Why do I have to go to work? It's such a drag. I knew I slept too much" or "I didn't sleep enough," or whatever the sequence of events you might be experiencing. Sound familiar? A thought arises and subsides, and there's a space. This is the way it functions—it arises and it subsides, and there's space.

The purpose of this Quantum exercise is to bring you back into the space between thoughts. If there's anything that you identify with, it will limit you. "I like blue shirts, I like red shirts, I like tall women, I like short women," whatever it may be. Whatever you believe will limit you, or you could say anything that you identify with or feel attached to, will eventually lead to a contracted and limited experience of oneself.

Webster defines contemplation as "to look at or view with continued attention; observe thoughtfully, to consider or reflect upon." Throughout the book, when I use the word contemplate I mean "to *consider* and *reflect*".

Quantum Contemplation

Look into your experience and ask yourself, "Who is it that is always witnessing my mind? Who is it that is always there watching?" The answer is "I am".

There is no answer to the question "From where does this thought arise?" However, notice what happens as you ask that question and look for the space from which each thought arose. To where does that thought arise? If a thought comes by that says "I don't understand," you immediately say, "That's me. That's me because I don't understand. I never understood anything"—this is my story. The benefit is that the more you can observe yourself, the more distance between you and the thought develops. This begins to enhance the ability to choose your identifications rather than finding yourself automatically in the rapids of your mind. Observation gives you a lever or wedge between you and your mind.

The first time I worked with a married couple, the woman stopped her inquiring, looked at me and said, "I'm trying to think of something to say—I'm always trying to think of something to say." I interjected, "That's the story of your life," and she answered, "Yes." The thought "I should say something" went by and she identified it as herself. She would then run all her internal dialogue about how and why she never knew what she should say. A helpful process for her is to ask, "From where does that thought arise?" No matter what thought comes to your awareness, ask, "From where does that thought arise?" "I feel afraid to get started?" Ask yourself, "From where does this thought arise?" As other thoughts arise, keep asking, "From where does this thought arise?"

There is a thought called "I'm afraid," when you first came to the thought "I'm afraid," you identified with it and said, "That's me." Then suddenly your mind said, "I'm afraid *because* I don't have enough money," "I'm fearful because my relationship is screwed up," "I'm afraid because—" whatever it is. The minute you identify with any thought, you have all of the associated psycho-emotional reactions such as "I'm afraid." And your mind will give you a thousand reasons why you're afraid.

• •

Practice

To begin experimenting with this exercise, very gently let your eyes close. Each time a thought comes through, begin to ask yourself, "From where does this thought arise?"

• •

Quantum Exercise 4

• •

When a thought arises, ask yourself "*To whom* does this thought arise?" You will probably answer "To me." Then ask a second question: "Who is *this I*?"

"Keep the attention fixed on finding out the source of the "I" thought by asking, as each thought arises, to whom the thought arises. If the answer is "I get the thought" continue the enquiry by asking "Who is *this* "I." (Godman, 1985)

This is reminiscent of an old Indian approach of asking yourself "Who am I?" I did this inquiring for some time and kept getting more and more answers, which I then had to look at. Asking "Who is *this* I," moved me from "being" the thoughts—to observing the thoughts.

Observe your experience and repeat this process with each new thought. Notice the rising and falling of your breathing as you notice the rising and subsiding of the

different thoughts. As each thought arises, ask "To whom does this thought arise?", receive the answer "To me," and ask "Who is this I?"

You can also do this exercise quite effectively with another person. Sitting comfortably facing one another, one person begins by reporting a thought—"I feel funny doing this, I'd rather be outside," for example. The partner responds "To whom does this thought arise?" "To me," the first person naturally responds. "And who is this I?" queries the partner.

● ●

The purpose of this exercise is to begin to sense the difference between the "transient i's"—the changing identities associated with the different thoughts—and the steadying presence of the observer, which is always there, watching the mental parade. Without the observer, most of us go through the day flip-flopping back and forth amidst the waves of our thoughts. With the crest of each wave, we bob around at the mercy of the next wave.

An example: My alarm clock rings one morning, as it usually does, at 7:00 a.m. My first thought is, "I'm tired, I don't want to go to work." Instantaneously, I identify with the thought. In essence, I say to myself *"That's me—*I'm tired and I don't want to go to work."

After breakfast, a thought goes by, "I can hardly wait to tell Jack about my new idea for redesigning the training program." The same instantaneous identification takes place. *"That's me—*I have a great idea." Suddenly I feel energized and excited about my work.

Now it's 10:30 in the morning and a thought goes by, "I'm bored, why did I pick this career?" The nonverbalized identification kicks in—*"That's me—*I'm bored with my job." By noon I'm thinking, "I'm really looking forward to my meeting with Lillian—she's so stimulating to discuss new ideas and problems with." The implicit aspect of this dynamic is the same as in all the other instances: *"That's me—*I can't wait to talk to Lillian."

The next morning I wake up and look at my partner lying next to me and a thought goes by that says, "Why am I in this relationship?" Instantaneously identify with the thought: *"That's me—*"I want out of this relationship"..."I never should have gotten married." I could have so much more freedom." At breakfast I find that I am having a pleasant conversation with my partner. "This is really comforting," I think, "I like the stability."

During my mid-morning break, an attractive person walks past me in the corridor and I think, "I'd like to meet that person," followed by, "Maybe I'd be better off single...I could do exactly what I want..."

Sound tediously familiar?

The point of this example is to provide a sense of how the mind is always changing its mind, so to speak. When we identify with each and every thought, we ride an emotional roller coaster. Learning to observe and witness takes more and more of the tumult out of daily experience. The mind will still generate its geyser of ever-changing wants, opinions, and demands, but the *you* that observes your mind will develop an equilibrium. Instead of whipping through the day on a roller coaster, you will begin to glide on still waters.

Is there an answer to the question "Who is *this* I?" No. The point of the exercise is to move you out of the typical, transient experience of being the subject who is identified with each and every varying state ("I am no good") to a less familiar experience of yourself as an observing presence. The experience of "I"—which is generally so personal, so subjective, so attached—becomes more objectified and the intense feelings of identification begin to lessen.

In Quantum Exercise 2, we learned to experience the space or emptiness between two thoughts. Here you are learning to experience oneself as being separate from the comings and going of the mind.

By practicing the exercises in Level 1, in which you learn to experience the space (the changeless implicate order) between your thoughts and identifications (the ever-changing explicate order), you can begin to experience a sense of equilibrium rather than riding the waves of your ever-changing mind.

After I had been observing my thoughts for a period of time, I went to my teacher, Nisargadatta Maharaj, and said "I feel like I'm thinking more and more when I witness all these thoughts coming and going. Am I thinking more or observing more?"

He said, "You're observing more, so you're more aware of

more of your thoughts. Therefore, it feels uncomfortable. It's just a phase."

I said, "It's a *long* phase!"

Anything you believe about yourself is limiting. I feel good, I feel lousy, I'm too tall, I hate myself, I can't cope, I'm no good at relationships—each of these we experience as separate psycho-emotional states with separate waves of feelings, sensations, and emotions. In quantum terms, however, each thought is a part-(icle) of energy surrounded by space and, as mentioned earlier, can be experienced as a wave of energy arising out of and subsiding back into emptiness. Actually, the word *quantum comes from the word quanta, meaning energy packet.* In the same way, each experience is like a packet of energy. This is why we can experience thoughts, feelings, emotions, etc. with such *"energetic force."* If we were to look through our quantum lens, we would see that all the particles or waves look alike. The implication of this quantum reality on a psychological level is that all the oscillating emotional and psycho-logical states (*part*-icles or waves) we experience as being so remarkably different are, in fact, not fundamentally different. To the degree to which we identify with the states (or particles/waves) as being different, we go up and down emotionally.

A workshop participant once commented, "It seemed as though I was witnessing and going into the space primarily, and then there were thoughts going on, but I couldn't pay attention to them. Rather than focusing on them, it was as if I had gotten beyond them." Another trainee commented, "When I use the approach, I experi-ence my thoughts slowing down in a rhythm. The shift is subtle, but I do experience a distancing from whatever the thought and internal experience was."

Quantum Exercise 5

● ●

Whenever a thought arises ask, "Who is witnessing?" Answer "I am."

If you look at your experiences, you'll see that you are always witnessing your thoughts. In fact, if you ask yourself, "Who has always been there witnessing what-

ever has happened to me," it is clear that *you were.* The question to ask yourself in this exercise is "Who is witnessing." Answer "I am." This exercise can be done by pairing up with a partner. Person A says whatever comes into his/her mind. Person B asks "who is witnessing that?" Person A replies "I am." Whatever comes up, person B continues to ask "who is the witness?" Person A replies, "I am." Do this for about five minutes each.

The next step is to sit quietly and ask yourself, "who is witnessing?" Answer "I am."

● ●

One person in a workshop commented, "My experience was that of realizing that there is two of me: a witness and the other being who continually has thoughts." Another workshop participant commented, "It was so obvious that I can't believe I overlooked that I was always there no matter what thoughts or feeling came and went...very freeing."

Quantum Exercise 6

● ●

Sit with your eyes closed, and notice all the transient "i's" that come and go. For example, "i feel good," "i feel bad," "i like myself," "i don't like myself."

Focus your attention on the permanent I, the I or witness that observes all the transient "i's."

Practice

Possible format for rotating group facilitator:

"Notice the sounds around you. Feel your body pressed up against the seat. Begin to focus on the thought-free I, the presence behind all of the pseudo-i's. Notice what-

ever sounds are around you, and again focus your
attention on the thought-free I, the presence behind all
the pseudo-i's. Very gently, bring your awareness back
to the room, and, whenever you're ready, let your eyes
open."

● ●

In the next exercise *anything* that comes into your awareness
should be seen as an object. So, "I feel good" can be *viewed as an
object* and witnessed. "I like being here" can be *viewed as an object.*
"I wish I weren't here" can be *viewed as an object.* "I feel a lot of
love" can be *viewed as an object* and witnessed. I remember in the
first class in the series I taught, a student said that he was feeling a
lot of bliss with this exercise. He said that *when he viewed the bliss
as an object* and observed, *he shifted into a space* where he had
never been before. Usually, we take a feeling like bliss and go, "I'm
in bliss," and later crash. He was able to move it to an object and
observe.

See what the experience is. And if something says, "This is a
neat experience," then you want to reduce "This is a neat experience" to an object. The next thought is "I really like doing this, that
feels neat" and you start feeling "neat." *Move "I feel neat" to an
object.* Whatever it is, reduce it to an object.

Quantum Exercise 7

● ●

Any thought can be objectified.

When a thought arises, make it into an object and
witness it. Make anything that comes into your awareness into an object and *observe.*

Practice

Possible format for facilitator:

"Begin by sitting and watching your breathing. What-

ever experience or thought comes through your awareness, reduce that to an object so that you're witnessing
that thought or experience that comes through your
awareness. Very gently, view it as an object. Whatever
thought or feelings or experiences that you are having,
view them as an object to be witnessed."

• ❖

A workshop participant once said to me after this exercise, "I
was immediately drawn into a beingness or an energy and then that
energy expanded. I was able to disappear into that energy so that all
that was there was the energy. I was not there." It's really easy just
to witness. All you have to do is be, it really requires no effort.

Quantum Contemplation

Contemplate what it would be like to be free of all thoughts.

A student commented, "I saw the thoughts as hooks in my mind;
some seemed harder to release than others, and I realized they were
more like fish hooks, like little barbs. It was pretty interesting."
Another student said, "I had a hard time when you said to be free of
all thought constructs. It was as if as soon as I was given permission
to be free, I went through all these tapes about why I couldn't be free.
I couldn't imagine being free." I told this student to notice beliefs
such as "I can't be free."

I was sitting with a yoga teacher, Baba Prakashananda in
Bombay. He and I were the only ones in the room. All of a sudden,
he began sending me a lot of energy. He was looking at me, and my
body started to feel really hot. I felt incredible psychic agony, I felt
like I had to hold onto the rug. I had decided that he was doing
something; I didn't know what it was but I wanted to. The energy
got more and more intense, and I thought I was going to go crazy.
He was looking down at me, which of course made it even worse.
I waited for something to emerge from beneath my usual awareness.
What came by was, "*I'm sorry that I am.*" I looked at it, observed
it, and watched it subside (disappear). I was in a completely

different state. What was true was that I had walked around unconsciously in my life saying, "I'm sorry, I'm sorry that I am." That had been my pattern, and I had walked around experiencing that. There are two reasons I tell this story. First, I tell it to point out the process of things emerging from underneath our usual awareness—from that ninety percent of our minds that is "underwater" like an iceberg, Meher Baba's analogy I cited earlier in this book. "I'm sorry that I am" came up from under the water; I saw it as an object and then could let go of it. Basically, it seems that you cannot let go of something until you know what it is. Second, when I started working in groups, I noticed that the issues and patterns were heightened more because the energy is a little bit stronger in groups than when one is alone.

The first step in actually experiencing the underlying unity of the quantum universe is to get in touch with the changeless observer that is always present. Indeed, one of the most important understandings in quantum physics is that space predominates throughout the universe. The one thing we all share is this unified space. While contacting something so vast seems like a tall order, it can be achieved by taking the step of observing your thoughts, identifications, and emotions and experiencing the space between them, or by becoming aware that you are the observer of your mind. As you do this over time, you feel an increasing sense of equilibrium as you allow yourself to perceive the space between each "thought-wave" as it arises and subsides. Experiencing the space between our thoughts eventually leads to a loosening of all the boundaries we put around things, ideas, people, and so on. And as the boundaries loosen, our level of comfort increases.

The second Level takes us further into the boundless region of Quantum Consciousness as we begin to work with emotions as energy.

FOUR

THE ENERGY OF
EMOTIONS

Few of us could deny the power of emotions. Just notice how this energy *takes over* your body, your thoughts, your reactions, and your decision-making process. Throughout history philosophers have attempted to explain the irrational nature of emotions. In the 1960's, the human potential movement began to suggest multitudes of ways to handle these feelings and emotional states, which appear to have a life of their own.

In the last chapter we explored and, I hope, experienced ourselves as the witness or observer of our thoughts and emotions. This chapter brings us to another *quantum jump* beginning to experience our emotions, feelings and the rest of the world as made of energy.

Throughout our life certain sensations in our body are experienced as good and desirable. We love happiness and joy. Other emotions, however, are said to be bad, unpleasant and undesirable, like anger, hurt, fear, or sadness. As we move closer to a Quantum understanding and begin to employ the use of our *quantum lens* more, we can begin to appreciate that the world, as noted physicist David Bohm suggests, is made of energy. How then can we apply this principle in our daily lives to help us feel more connected to everything else and less in pain, particularly pertaining to unwanted emotional states like anger, sadness, and hate.

Level 2

The universe is made of energy.

To begin our journey it is important to trace back the unwanted feelings to determine their origin and what emotions are composed of. Later in the chapter, Quantum exercises will be presented that can be done individually, in pairs, or in a group, so this awareness becomes more experiential and less intellectual.

What does Emotion mean? E means outward. Therefore E-motion means outward motion. When we look at an unwanted emotion such as anger, we notice that when you remove the label of anger from this experience you are probably feeling just a movement of energy passing through your physical body. What has happened is that this energy which would normally just pass through your body, is labeled anger, with probably a "bad," or "I shouldn't feel" definition attached to it. The problem arises when the labeling takes place. Once you, as the observer, label this energy in any way, you put a boundary around it, you contract it, because you consider it bad, unwanted and resist it. This labeling process keeps the experience contracted, bounded, and creates an air of resistance, as opposed to seeing it as energy, which is the basic substance of this E-motion. In psychotherapy, often a client is asked to reframe a problem, feeling, or emotion into a solution.

For example, a client that feels anxious might be given suggestions by the therapist to see the anxiety as a motivator, or an internal barometer that is letting him/her know that something needs to get done. This reframing technique adds a new label called "motivator" over the original label called "anger". Hence, the feeling is seen differently, but generally you feel neither closer to yourself nor more connected to others. The process of seeing everything as made of energy is actually a process of *de-labeling* or de-framing, taking off all labels and seeing emotions as energy—their most basic substance.

In the last chapter, we explored the wave-like function of thoughts or feelings. In this chapter we will explore David Bohm's energy function, "the universe is an unfolding and enfolding of energy, space, mass and time." In the chapters to follow, we will look at the space, mass, and time aspects. Each aspect of consciousness can be seen as a rite of passage, because as we let go of, or become less ridged in, one aspect of consciousness, it frees us to go onto the next.

But now, first things first. While teaching a seminar in 1983, a participant asked me how I came to this philosophy. In 1976, I was 26 years old and had been inspired to move to India and live in a monastery to continue my inner search. Unfortunately for me, the place I chose to live was a celibate community. Being 26 with full hormones functioning, I was like a poster I saw of a yogi, sitting in meditation, and above the yogis' head was a cartoon bubble fantasy of having sex with a woman. It was like Mark Twain's old saying, "Marriage has many pains, but celibacy has no pleasures." Being a horny celibate, I very soon realized that repression, repetition of mantra, working physically or taking on a sex-is-bad belief system not only didn't help, but aggravated the situation. It was like being asked not to think of a monkey. Of course, when you are asked not to think of something, you have to keep the monkey there, in order to know what *not* to think about.

One day, however, I experienced a sexual fantasy. I realized that since nobody was there in my room, then all these pleasant feelings were coming from inside me. I turned my attention away from the fantasy, and focused on the sensations themselves as energy. A profound happening occurred—I went into a deep sense of peace, comfort and bliss. This was awesome because in the past if I had a fantasy, I would go chase after the fantasy outside myself by thinking that it could give me these pleasant sensations or feelings. To realize that they came from inside of me and that the sensations were mine, and to be able to see them as energy, *transformed* my entire experience. Later, I found a passage from an ancient text, the Vijnanabhairava:

"Since the sexual pleasure is obtained simply by memory even in the absence of a woman, it is evident that the delight is inherent within. It is the delight apart from any woman (man) that one should meditate on." (Singh, 1979:67)

Several days later, it was about 5:30 a.m. and I was chanting Sanskrit mantras in a temple. It was mid-May in India and it was *hot*!! I began to feel angry, and my mind began to throw-up (no pun intended) pictures as to why I felt angry, i.e. "it's hot, I'm tired." Suddenly I put down my chanting book, and again turned my attention toward the anger itself. I saw the anger as made of energy. Quite suddenly there was a shift. The anger was transmuted. I began to pulsate with bliss. Looking back at this in 1983, I "realized" what Einstein had said, "that everything is emptiness and form is condensed emptiness." I was experiencing that pulsation or movement as the anger in its solid, palatable form, shifted back to energy and into the void. The form of anger (which was energy) moved back into the void (no energy).

I later found an ancient sanskrit text called the *Spanda Karikas*. "Spanda" means the divine pulsation and "karikas" translates as lessons, hence, *Lessons in the Divine Pulsation*. Paraphrased, it said, if at the moment of extreme anger, extreme sadness, or extreme joy, or if you are running for your life, if at that moment you could become introverted, you would experience spanda (the divine pulsation). What I did was to become introverted by taking my attention away from the object of my emotions, the story or reasons *why*, and focused on the feelings in my body *as energy*, and I experienced this pulsation. David Bohm says that the world is an unfolding and enfolding of energy, space, mass, and time. The pulsation was the unfolding and enfolding process that I was experiencing, as my emotions moved from manifest to unmanifest, manifest to unmanifest, in a rhythmic fashion.

"... so our reality is made up of a constant, rapid, back and forth shutting between our solid reality and the way-out reality which we share with everybody else. An expanded or higher state of consciousness implies an expansion of our psyche into space. So it can be said that in the oscillating movement of a pendulum, what you get is an oscillation of manifest/unmanifest, manifest/unmanifest, manifest/unmanifest, manifest/unmanifest, and what you're getting from that is nothing/something, nothing/something, nothing/something, nothing/something. And that can be defined in classic meditation as the space between two thoughts or the space between two breaths (Bentov, 1977:76).

Here Bentov is suggesting, that as we "observe," there is an oscillation, that can be likened to the movement of a pendulum. If you imagine the movement of a pendulum, the pendulum stops at one point, (space) and moves in the other direction and stops. This stopping point is the same as the space between two thoughts mentioned in the last chapter or one of the most widely used meditation techniques...the space between two breaths. In my emotional example, the pulsation I experienced occurred by de-labeling the E-motion as energy and allowing it (since no resistance was there), to move through me in a manifest/unmanifest way.

Quantum Exercise 8

• •

Focus on the space between two breaths.

This exercise is probably the most widely-used meditation technique I know. Although for many it may be "old hat," I review it here.

In this exercise, you are to just watch your breath. Watch your breath rise as you inhale. There will be a *space* before the inhale turns into an exhale, then you will exhale and there will be a *space* before your exhale turns into an inhale: inhale ... *space* ... exhale ... *space* ... inhale ... *space* ... exhale ... *space*. It will be the same space each time.

• •

Transmutation or
Transformation of E-motions

Transmutation can be defined as a change in condition or an alteration, as in qualities or states of mind. In this case, moving from the *dual awareness* to the *quantum awareness*. Noted Sufi teachers, G. I. Gurdjieff and P. D. Ouspensky suggested this work might be called "Psycho-transformism."

> "This idea of *work* is psychological transformation—the transformation of oneself. Transformation means changing one thing into a different thing." (Nicoll, 1984:50).

To the self-explorer, therapist, spiritual aspirant, or the individual exploring consciousness, it is imperative to understand why E-motions, events or situations are experienced the way they are. Anger without a label is energy in a different form than sadness. Sadness is energy in a different form than hate. Once experienced without labels, the judgement (I should not feel the anger), evaluation (anger is bad), and significance (What does feeling anger mean about me, or what will people think of me if I'm angry?), is removed, and we are all left with just energy. Energy with no label is hardly something to feel bad about, and one workshop participant remarked after doing the exercises, "There is no reason to resist the experience of anger, it is just energy, and just Is."

This is an effortless process. *Consciousness transmutes itself.* This is not a process of using effort to change one thing into another, because an individual "imagines" this or that is better. Here lie the subtle judgments, which lock the experience in space and time. Normally, psychology leaves us in the predicament of either expressing or repressing feelings that are judged through prior learnings as bad or unwanted. Transmutation affords the opportunity to add a third alternative to expression, or repression, namely transmutation. By seeing the E-motion as energy, transformation occurs.

Merely by observing or watching E-motions, thoughts and feelings as they are (namely energy), the "experience" transmutes itself. In the Sufi work of Gurdjieff and Ouspensky, self-observation yields transformation. From my own experience, self-observation only yielded more self-observation and more internal states to observe.

From a Quantum Psychology perspective, we are adding on, to self-observation, the de-labeling or de-framing process, which is experiencing E-motions as energy. In order for anything to exist in the physical universe, it must have energy.

Quantum Contemplations

If emotions, such as anger, fear, etc. did not have energy in them, would they be a problem?

Can a problem state exist, if it has no energy?

The Quantum Touch

The add-on to these profound Sufi teachings is the Quantum touch, namely observing the E-motions as energy. This de-labeling or de-framing causes a transmutation in the experience of E-motions and is where the transformation takes place. The Quantum touch acts like a philosopher's stone. In alchemy, the metaphor of the philosopher's stone transforms metals into gold (your true self). In the same way, observing E-motions as energy acts as a philosopher's stone, returning you to yourself (*The Gold*). This is transformation. Noted psychiatrist Carl Jung, M.D. felt strongly about the use of emotions as energy. Jung suggested:

> "In the intensity of the emotional disturbance itself lies the value, the energy which he should have at his deepest disposal in order to remedy the state of reduced adaptation." (Jung, 1960).

What follows are the steps to transmute thoughts, feelings, E-motions, and sensations. You, as the observer of an experience put the label on. The following Quantum exercises can be used to take the label off and experience experiences as they are. The exercises can be done in a group, in pairs, or individually. The following are E-motions which are frequently defined by people as problem states. The purpose is to give us a chance to practice the exercises and notice what occurs. Please note that Quantum Psychology is not a spectator sport; experiencing is its cornerstone. Practice is essential.

The purpose of the following exercise is to help you begin to transmute your experiences so that psycho-emotional energies are experienced as pure energy which appear in different shapes or forms. This allows us to move forward into a deeper sense of self, since psychic energy is no longer drained off in resistance to a created label. As mentioned earlier, if I label energy as anger, "which is bad," then I will resist my own created label. Throughout this group of Quantum exercises we are asked to de-label and experience E-motions as made of energy.

Quantum Exercise 9

• •

Working with your fear.

Step I:	**Recall a story or memory about when you felt fear.**
Step II:	**Allow the fear to manifest.**
Step III:	**Notice where in your body the fear is occurring.**
Step IV:	**Take your attention off the story as to why you feel fear.**
Step V:	**Put your attention and focus on the fear itself; now de-label it seeing it as energy.**
Step VI:	**If you are working in a group, make eye contact with different group members, seeing the energy inside of them as being made of the same energy as the energy within yourself.**

When you feel afraid, your mind gives you many reasons why you're afraid. Normally people focus their attention on the story about why they are afraid. In this exercise you turn your attention from the story and put it on the fear itself. Where is the fear in your body? Begin to focus your attention on the fear itself.

Practice

A rotating group leader may consider reading this slowly, as a format for practice.

"Begin by remembering a past event or something that you're imagining will happen in the future that is associated with fear. It could have been last week, it could have been last month, it could have been last year. Let a memory of something you're afraid of come into your mind. Notice what kind of clothes you are wearing in the story, what color they are. Notice if there are any other people in the memory or movie in you mind's eye. Experience any sounds you hear in the movie. Observe the feelings of fear you have and where it is in your body. Let your movie or story really develop. Now, as it reaches a level of intense feeling, very gently, take your attention from the movie and move your attention to the fear itself, or the emotion itself. Notice where in your body your feeling of fear is. Focus your attention on the fear in your body. Where is it? Every time your mind wants to go to the story or movie about why you're afraid, move it gently to the feelings of the fear itself. Begin to view that fear simply as energy. *Continue to see the fear as energy.* Remember, your task is to see it as it is, not to change it, move it, or offer it to God. Just see it as energy. *DON'T try to change it.*"

● ●

Why? Because if *you are trying to get rid of or change anything, you are resisting it.* In the Sufi tradition the energy is referred to as the scorpion, and the label placed on the energy as the perfume. To add a label to pure energy is like adding perfume to a scorpion. Why? Because you will experience the label or perfume not the underlying energy.

> Therefore it is said, "Whoever would perfume a scorpion will not thereby escape its sting."—Bahaudin (Shah, 1978).

Therefore, allow the de-labeled energy to have it's own outward motion, without your interrupting it with a judgement ("I shouldn't have it"), evaluation ("It is bad"), or significance ("What does this mean about me?").

By allowing the natural, outward motion of energy to occur, the energy passes right through you. In essence, you can get out of the way and allow the energy to do what it does.

In the late 60's and early 70's, the heyday of the human potential movement, neurosis, (self-defeating behavior) could best be summed up as being caused by an interruption in the outward motion. To illustrate, a child feels energy passing through it and begins to make noise. Mom or dad says, "Don't be angry." Here is an external interruption in the outward motion of energy. The parents have labeled this sound as yelling, anger, bad. This child learns to label this energetic outward motion as anger and bad and begins to interrupt his/her own outward motion. In many human potential movement therapies, i.e., Gestalt, psychodrama, bio-energetics, etc., the therapy is based on completing or finishing the "unfinished business," by "not interrupting" and "going with" the feelings through expressing. Here, we are taking the labels with all their meanings off of the E-motion, seeing it as energy and allowing the energy to do what it does. This is feeling the emotions, which is subtly different than expressing feelings. This allows the interruption to be re-solved.

Years ago I was taking a class in Feldenkrais Awareness through Movement from Carl Ginsburg, a Feldenkrais trainer. He said, "Learn to touch people without intention." I said, "Carl, that's not possible. If I touch someone, just by the act of touching there is an intention." He said, "It's a koan" (Zen question that is pondered and designed to bring one to a particular state of consciousness). I spent time with this and came to understand what Carl Ginsburg was saying. I applied this to Quantum Psychology: you watch the Emotions as energy *just to watch* and notice what happens, without their being an *intention* or a goal in mind of it changing or getting rid of it. You see emotions as energy. Just to do it—*without any intention!!!*

When doing the exercises, watch and notice what occurs as you witness E-motions as made of energy.

As you watch the E-motion, begin to feel it as energy. See the emotion as energy moving in your system. If the emotion has unpleasant associations, the energy has a tendency to get stronger and stronger because it was more repressed. Gradually the energy starts moving on its own. It might take five or ten minutes, maybe five days or five seconds. *There's no rush and no goal*, only de-labeling, and watching the emotions as energy.

As an example, when you are working with yourself on some deep emotional experience, seeing it as energy becomes something you can practice. You might do it in your spare time. Just stay with it and eventually something will happen.

Years ago, while living in Santa Cruz, I received a phone call that was very upsetting. I had never experienced an anxiety attack, although, as a psychotherapist, I had helped people with that problem many times. After the phone call, my body turned cold, my heart was pounding, and I was frozen and in terror. I truly did not know what it was. Kristi, being a good partner, said, "You're having an anxiety attack." Needless to say, I fought it, resisted it, covered myself with blankets. It was horrible. To make it even worse, I went and saw the movie *Casualties of War*. I guess I was a glutton for punishment.

Later on I thought to myself, "I can hardly wait for my next anxiety attack." Why? Because there was so much energy in it to *use*. Sure enough about two weeks later, BANG, heart palpitations, dry mouth, body frozen in terror. This time, however, keeping a certain "observing presence," I realized what was happening. I lay down on the floor, and focused my attention on my body, the fear, the sensations as energy. My attitude was "take me wherever." After a short period of time, I felt my heart open. I was vulnerable, very connected to myself and I experienced a beautiful state. This is the potential of this kind of practice.

All these exercises are designed to transform your habitual awareness from focusing on the *story of why*, to focusing on the Emotion itself, as made of energy, whether the emotion is pleasant or unpleasant. The underlying assumption we are using is the concept that everything is energy. Your E-motions are energy—the chair is energy, everything is energy in different shapes and forms.

One workshop participant in North Carolina reported that as he turned his attention away from the story and onto the feeling itself, the energy moved down his legs and out his feet. "What was interesting," he said, "was that I couldn't have planned that, or even thought of that as a possibility." I said, "That's' right, you watch the E-motions as energy with *no intention*, just with interest and curiosity. Notice what happens."

One workshop participant said, "This feels hard and like work." I replied, "It is a practice—you're changing a *habitual pattern* of focusing on the story of why you feel what you feel, to the feelings themselves. You're changing a habit." We have all been trained to focus on the story or reason *why* we are feeling what we are feeling. As you practice, you will begin to focus quite naturally on the energy itself. It is comparable to learning a sport. At first you might feel very awkward, but after a while you can play the sport without thinking about it. It starts happening in and of itself. When you get into a swimming pool, you don't have to think about swimming, you swim. You don't have to think about holding your breath when you go under water, you do it. As you practice, this becomes quite natural.

Quantum Exercise 10

● ●

Working with sadness.

In this exercise, working with the label and experience of sadness as energy is explored. We'll begin to remember some past situation in which you experienced some sadness. Next, move your attention from the story of why you're sad, or why you're feeling E-motional, to the energy of sadness itself.

Step I: Recall a story or memory about when you felt sadness.

Step II: Allow the sadness to manifest.

Step III: Notice where in your body the sadness is occurring.

Step IV: Take your attention off the story as to why you feel sadness.

Step V: Put your attention and focus on the sadness itself, de-labeling it and seeing it as energy. If any thoughts, impressions, or the story comes up—see it as energy.

Step VI: If you are working in a group, make eye contact with different group members, seeing the energy within them as being made of the same energy as the energy within yourself.

The rotating group leader may consider the following format.

Practice

Sit for about ten minutes. Start by feeling your body, how it's placed. Watch your breath rising and falling. Begin to allow a remembrance to come into your awareness pertaining to sadness. What people are involved in the story? Where are you in the story? Notice if there are sounds and emotions.

For a few minutes begin to allow that E-motion to become stronger and stronger. Notice the feelings associated with the story. Gently, move your awareness from the story, the reasons or people in your story,

toward the E-motion itself. See where the feeling is in
your body. Notice its size, color, and whether it has a
sound. Focus all your attention on the E-motion rather
than the story. Witness the E-motion as energy.

• •

A workshop participant asked me, "This seems very contrived,
so how do I apply this in everyday situations?" I said, "In the context
of the workshop, it is often contrived because you may or may not
be able to bring up sadness." The idea is to practice, so that while
living your daily life and things come up, you can observe and use
the energy as fuel, to reconnect you back to yourself. In this way
every experience becomes the fuel or energy and an opportunity to
connect by seeing and experiencing the E-motion as energy, rather
than the ordinary experience of separation and disconnection when
we resist and label the E-motion."

Quantum Exercise 11

• •

Working with anger.

Step I: Recall a story or memory when you felt
             angry.

Step II: Allow the energy to manifest.

Step III: Notice where in your body the anger is
             occurring.

Step IV: Notice the size and shape of the anger.

Step V: Take your attention away from the story as
             to why you are angry.

Step VI: De-label the anger, see it as energy and
             merge with it.

• •

Before we go into the experience of working with anger, I think it is important for me to recount a story of what happened to me while in India, and why I have added another step to the process.

In 1979, while living in the monastery in India, the environment was set up to "increase the energy" by avoiding talking and sex, and little food was available, etc. There was a lot of emotional pain since nobody there had a way to escape. I'm sure we can all relate to feeling anger and running to get chocolate, or to a movie, or having sex to handle the emotional state. With no escape, one day I felt so much anger that my body felt like it was in flames and I was on fire. My friend Mark Mordin, who had lived in India for twelve years, said, "Be the fire, rather than the fuel." What I did was merge with the fire rather than being the one that was being burned. Quite instantly, I felt calm, relaxed and more centered. Since then, while working with clients or in workshops, I suggest to people who are feeling overwhelmed by anger to notice where in their body they are experiencing this emotion, and to notice its size and shape since emotions are made of energy in different shapes and forms. For example anger is a different form of energy than love. This means that although the anger is made of the same energy as the love, it's shape or the form it takes is different because of the label. Finally, I ask people to *be* the emotion *completely*. Merge with the emotion as energy.

The results have been amazingly powerful. One client recently was experiencing anxiety attacks. I asked her, "Where in your body do you experience the anxiety?" She replied, "My chest." I said, "Notice the size and dimensions of the anxiety." She said, "It has a funny not quite oval shape." I said, "Be the anxiety completely. Rather than being the one feeling anxious, be the anxiety as energy." She replied, "Wow, I feel more centered, more relaxed, more myself."

This exercise focuses on anger, but if another emotion comes in, you can also use that one. Here is a format for the rotating group facilitator to consider.

• •

Practice

Format for rotating group leader:

Remember a scene. It could have been last year, it could have been five years ago, it could have been ten years ago. Let the E-motion called anger to come into your awareness. As you watch this scene and yourself in it, look around and notice other people and sounds. Notice what the feeling is or what the sensations in your body are. Your awareness might be pulled out a little by the sounds around you, but again, focus on the movie, the story. Allow the emotion or sensations of anger to begin to emerge and come to the surface as you watch the remembered experience. Notice where in your body it is: in your chest, or wherever it might be. Notice its shape or its size. Now, take your attention away from the story and focus on the anger itself as made of energy.

Begin to focus your awareness on this anger rather than on the story and reasons why you're angry. *Focus on the anger itself*. As you watch the anger, you'll notice that you'll begin to see it as energy in a compacted form. Notice its size or how it might move or not move. At first it might get more intense, but as you continue to watch it as energy in compact form, notice what *happens*. If thoughts or the story comes up—see it as energy. Now merge with and *be* the anger as energy, rather than the one who is angry. Focus on that energy as you.

When you are ready, very gently allow yourself to come back to the room.

• •

A student once reported: "My anger was rectangular, and there were two holes on either side." I replied, "If your anger has a particular shape or color, focus on that, and *be* the anger as energy;

notice what happens." Carl Jung, M.D. utilized emotional states as pathways,

> "The whole procedure is a kind of enrichment and clarification of the affect whereby the affect and the content are brought nearer to consciousnes…The emotional disturbance can also be dealt with in another way not by clarifying it intellectually, but by giving it a *visible shape*." (Rossi, 1986:85-96)

Quantum Exercise 12

● ●

Working on jealousy.

Step I: Recall a story or memory when you felt jealous.

Step II: Allow the energy to manifest.

Step III: Notice where in your body the jealousy is occurring.

Step IV: Notice the size and shape of the jealousy.

Step V: Take your attention away from the story as to why you are jealous.

Step VI: De-label the jealousy and see it as energy. If any thoughts, impressions, associations or the story comes up—see it as energy.

● ●

Here the work remains the same. Continue to focus your attention on the E-motion as energy rather than on the story of why the E-motion is present. We are again assuming that all thoughts and E-motions are energy in a different form. First, we'll bring up a story of jealousy. Then we'll move away from the film and move our attention to the feeling of jealousy. If you don't have any conscious feeling of jealousy, use another E-motion.

We are planting seeds, so that when you are jealous a week from now or two years from now, you'll switch your attention to experiencing the emotion itself. Once it happens for you, it will start a whole chain of events.

I was really upset with some people about a month and a half ago. A friend said to me, "Why focus on the people? Why not focus on the feelings?" I did and walked through the steps; once again the energy transformed (shifted) itself.

• •

Practice

Format for rotating group facilitator to consider:

Remember a scene in which you felt you had every right to be jealous. Notice who is involved in the scene that you're watching. Notice the temperature in the scene in your memory, or if you can experience any voices or sounds. Let the film roll. Notice the feelings that arise as you watch the film. Watch the film and the story called jealousy. Notice any sensations.

Very gently, pull your awareness away from the film. See if you can find where in your body you are experiencing the feelings called jealousy. Notice the size and shape of the emotion. Begin to witness the jealousy as energy in a different form, then a chair, or your arm. If any thoughts, or impressions come up—see them as energy. See if there is a color or a temperature to the energy. View it as energy, listen to its sound, watch it. Continue to watch whatever feelings are going on inside you and try to view them as energy. Notice its dimensions and shape. Merge with and *be* the emotion as energy.

• •

I have found that it is surprisingly difficult sometimes to pull your attention away from the story and onto the feelings, because you feel so justified. Sometimes my students have felt they got "stuck" at some point in the process. If this happens, I suggest that you continue by focusing on the "stuckness" as made of energy.

Workshop participants have often asked me about repressing emotions as opposed to expressing them. There's repressing, which means sitting on your jealousy or anger. There's expressing—two opposite sides of the same thing. Then there's allowing the energy to be. The quantum approach gives us the third option, the awareness that what you are experiencing is energy.

One workshop participant said, "When I'm really angry, I don't think. I know I'm angry, but the thought of doing something about it rather than letting the motion picture go through my mind for hours and hours doesn't dawn on me." I said, "*This is a practice.*" Right now the film is going on and on and on and on. Our hope is that two weeks from now it will only go on and on. And then it will go on. In other words, we want to recognize your pattern and catch your pattern earlier and earlier.

Say you always pick lousy relationships. Suddenly, ten years later, you say, "Gee, I did it again." And you pick another relationship and it's five years later. When you pick it up again it's two years later, then it's one year later. We hope you work it out before you die! The same goes for handling emotions; the more you practice inner transmutation the easier it gets, and the earlier you will shift your attention."

A student brought his experience with the teachings of G. I. Gurdjieff, a Sufi master, to try to be awake and to observe constantly what one does. "When the feeling of anger or whatever came up," he said, "we'd give it a name like John. When it came up later, we could say: 'Here comes John again.'"

I commented, "In psychosynthesis, that's called using subpersonalities. Oh, there's John. John's running his number. There's Fred." There is even a therapy called "name therapy", and one called "voice dialogues'. You can give names to all the different parts of your personality and then watch them do their numbers, or you can even talk with each one. Using that technique helps to get some distance on them. There is another level, however, because you are beyond these sub-personalities. As will be demonstrated in the next chapter, you are also the creator of the sub-personalties.

Using names is a psychosynthesis way of working on feelings. You could draw pictures of them and put them on your wall to get more in touch with them and know when they take over. Here in quantum, we are working with the basic substance: energy, rather than focusing on the part, sub-personality, I-dentity, or false self. We are focusing on what the emotion is made of, energy, its composition. This is where quantum psychology joins hands with psychology, Eastern traditions and quantum physics. In this approach, we synthesize East, Middle East, and West in this journey to uncover who we are.

Quantum Exercise 13

• •

Working with sexuality.

Step I: Recall a story or fantasy that made you feel sexual.

Step II: Allow the energy to manifest.

Step III: Notice where in your body the sexuality is occurring.

Step IV: Notice the size and shape of the sexual energy.

Step V: Take your attention away from the story as to why you feel sexual.

Step VI: De-label the sexual energy—and see it as energy. If any thoughts, impressions, associations or fantasies come-up—see them as energy.

• •

In this exercise we are looking at one of our favorite topics, sex. In order to explore this, it is time for us to add yet another ingredient to our quantum approach. In this step, we are going to begin to recognize that not only is the E-motion and sensation made of energy, so is the story or fantasy in our mind.

> "This is the first conscious shock and it is given the general description of remembering yourself. This state of consciousness leads to the transformation of impressions. Everyone is governed by his own set of reactons to impressions." (Nicoll,1984:52-54)

What Gurdjieff and Ouspensky are saying is that we focus on our impressions of life and never see life. We only see our impressions. In this exercise we will see our story (impressions) as made of energy, this will become the transformative agent.

To go even deeper, however, we are going to explore our skin boundaries as made of energy, as well as the chair, and expand this to include our entire universe.

Before we jump into this issue which carries us through so many feelings and memories, let us first look at it from different perspectives.

A Psychological Look

Wilhelm Reich, M.D., the creator of Reichian therapy, considered by many the father of body work, proposed a theory around sexuality as early as the 1940s, which has stood the test of time. Reich demonstrated that sex or the orgasm has a cycle, namely, tension, charge, discharge, relaxation. This can best be seen below.

Illustration 3

This can also be parallel to an emotional cycle and thought cycle presented in Chapter 3, where we feel anger or have a thought, we build up charge, we yell, and then feel relaxed. Reich believed that this was essential in maintaining the health of the individual and the body. Reich, it should be noted, caused so much controversy, that by the mid-to late 1950s, his books were burned by the Federal Food and Drug Administration in New York City. Reich was sent to Leavenworth prison. Wilhelm Reich actually died in prison. This is how controversial and highly charged the topic of sexuality is.

An Eastern Perspective

In India, and particularly in the last twenty-five years in the West, tantric yoga has become a recognized term referring to work with sexual energy. It should be noted, however, there are 112 yoga tantras or techniques to bring the practitioner into a greater "expansion of knowledge." I note this now because less than 1% of tantric yoga deals with sex. Yet, the issue of sexuality is so highly charged, that tantric yoga is *sold* in the West because of its association with sex, even though sex is less than 1% of it's actual practice. Furthermore, promotion of sex as tantra is a great marketing approach used by Indian "Gurus."

In working with sexual energy, however, and tantric yoga in its purest form, sexual energy is not seen as different from any other energy. In this way, "sexual energy" is not considered bad, unholy, or something that should be repressed. On the other hand, "sexual energy" is not seen as something that necessarily needs to be expressed. Normally, as mentioned earlier, we only have a polarity of choices: express (I will, I should) and repress (I shouldn't, I better not). This polarity, as all of us know, causes a conflict that has touched all of us at one time or another. In this approach however, sexual energy is allowed, recognized and observed, as what it is, energy in a different form than anger, or sadness or even physical objects (more about this later).

Tantric sex does not have a goal of orgasm. It is about what the definition of tantra is " the expansion of knowledge."

In Reich's orgasm cycle, the energy is discharged.

In tantric sex, however, there is tension, charge; your attention is turned around and the sensations are seen as energy. Notice what happens. Visually it can be seen and illustrated as follows.

Illustration 4

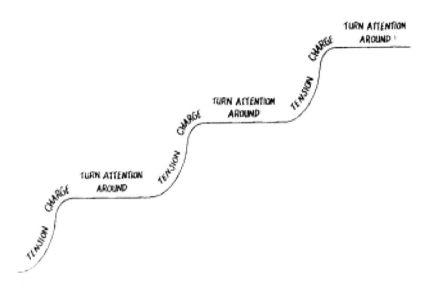

As you see the sexual sensation as energy, a plateau is reached. Then through sexual activity, the charge is built up again and at the moment of charge you turn your attention around and see the sensations as energy, another plateau. Working at higher and higher plateaus without discharging the energy causes an "expansion of knowledge" which is tantra.

Many books have been written on this subject, and I cannot say what happens for a woman. For a man, however, when he sees the sexual energy as energy and plateaus, he will generally loose his erection. Then the sexual process must continue on to build charge. The purpose of expansion of knowledge must be clear, otherwise there will be a discharge (orgasm) at an early stage.

There is a wonderful phrase from an ancient yoga text, paraphrased, "If at the moment of orgasm, one could become introverted (and see the sensations as energy), one would experience the divine pulsation." The thought that is omitted is, "if at the moment of orgasm, *you could remember.*'

A Quantum Look

Here we want to add to the steps mentioned at the beginning of the chapter. Physicist David Bohm said, "Everything inter*penetrates* everything else" (no pun intended). What this means, when we consider E-motions as well as the pleasant sensations of sex, is that not only is the sexual sensation energy, when de-labeled and seen as energy, but so are the skin boundaries of our body, the skin itself, our partner and what we call "I." Therefore, the quantum add-on to Reich and tantra is to not only see the sexual sensations as energy, but also your thoughts, fantasies in your mind, skin boundary, the world that surrounds the "I" and ultimately the "I" that is looking. In this way, our "individuality" begins to expand to include everything else.

So, you can experience your skin boundary as energy, the air as energy, the walls, your partner as energy, the state of New Mexico or any state you find yourself in, etc.

Illustration 5

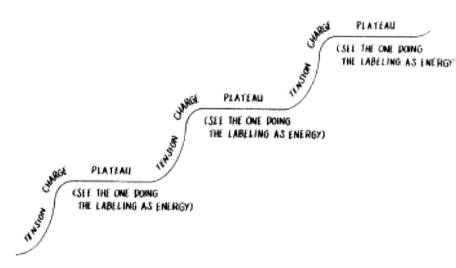

Here we have seen the background or context for working with sex. Now comes the fun part, practicing. Part 1 will be working with fantasies. Part 2 will be working with a sexual partner.

Quantum Exercise 14

● ●

Part 1: Sexual practice for individuals with fantasies, or as a guided practice in pairs or in a group. (Singh, 1979)

Step I: Either remember a time, notice your present sexual experience, or have a sexual fantasy.

Step II: Turn your attention away from the sexual fantasy and notice where in your body you are experiencing sexual sensations.

Step III: Experience the size and shape of the sexual feelings.

Step IV: De-label the sexual energy, seeing it as energy and merge with it.

Step V: Feel your skin boundaries as being made of the same energy as the "sexual" energy.

Step VI: Experience the air, the room, the floor, your chair, the rest of the universe including your thoughts as being made of the same energy.

● ●

If you have sexual fantasies (I know none of you do, but if you do) focus your attention on the sexual fantasy, or the story or the object of your sexual fantasy. Your mind is creating impressions of the sexual fantasy in some form or other. When I was celibate for about five years, I noticed that during the first three years I was going through incredible fantasies. Since the fantasies were still there, so were the bodily sensations. I had a difficult time for three years. All of a sudden I started to practice, and the practice changed my focus from putting my awareness on the fantasy to putting it on the energy itself. Where do I feel it? It's exactly the same as all of the E-motional issues, except that now we're working with a more "pleasant" one.

Rather than focusing on the story and trying to fulfill it outside of you, begin to observe that energy. This again simply means moving your attention away from the sexual fantasy into the energy itself. It's energy. It's not good or bad, right or wrong. It's energy.

I remember saying to an Indian teacher that I was having problems with my second chakra, (which is normally described as the sexual center in the body.) He said, "Only one chakra *energy*." It's all energy, only the mind wants to compartmentalize it and label it into chakras, higher and lower, etc.

● ●
Practice

Format that may be read by rotating group facilitator.

Let your eyes close and get yourself comfortable again. I'd like you to begin to develop a sexual fantasy. You can start by picking someone that you'd like to be with. Notice what they look like, whether there are any sounds. Let yourself watch your sexual fantasy. Notice if there are any smells or tastes, any sensations. Let the fantasy run for a moment.

Now move your attention from the movie of your sexual fantasy to the energy itself. Begin by noticing where in your body you feel that energy, where those sensations and those feelings are. Keep your attention on the energy itself. Where do you feel it, how do you feel it? Does it have a color or a shape or a sound? Keep your attention on the energy itself. If your attention goes toward the story, bring it back again, and watch the energy.

Notice the size and shape of the energy. *Be* the energy inside the shape. Now experience your skin boundary as being made of the same substance of which the shape is made. Experience the air around you, the chair, or any states of mind that "pop-up" as energy. Notice that even the "I" that's noticing and the E-motions are made of energy.

• •

Part 2: Quantum exercise with a sexual partner.

Step I: Notice your present sexual experience.

Step II: Notice part of your attention is on your sexual partner.

Step III: As the energy peaks, turn your attention away from your sexual partner and notice where in your body you are experiencing sexual sensations.

Step IV: Experience the size and shape of the sexual feelings, as you allow the sensations to build.

Step V: Merge with and *Be* the sensations as energy.

Step VI: Feel your skin boundaries as being made of the same energy as the sexual energy.

Step VII: Experience the air, the room, the floor, your chair, the rest of the universe including your thoughts as being made of the same energy.

Practice

Now, when you are with a partner focus on the partner, on the sensations, etc. (as if you won't be doing that). Then as the energy begins to peak, see the size and shape of the energy, where it is in your body, i.e. mouth, genitals, breasts. Merge with the energy, and experience your skin boundary as energy, the bed, the floor, the air, any thoughts, the room, and the rest of the universe. When you begin to plateau, just enjoy the experience. The process can then be repeated again, having "regular" sexual contact until an energetic charge is built up.

Then repeat the steps; focusing on the energy, its size and shape, merging with it, and experiencing as energy the skin, the air, etc.

• •

Recently, I had a client who complained of pre-mature ejaculation. He had fixated his entire at-(tension) on the tip of his penis. I suggested to him, and with the patience of his loving partner, that he begin to watch the sensations in his penis as *energy*. This afforded him greater and greater ability to *have* the energy and pleasure for himself, not to mention his partner. As he became more proficient in this way of working with himself, he began to be able to choose when to ejaculate, and allow it to occur at a higher plateau of consciousness.

In the early 1970s, a woman client in Los Angeles complained that she could have multiple orgasms, but she did not feel satisfied. Once again I suggested that she "build-up" energy, and then turn her attention around and see the sexual energy as just energy. She also practiced with her partner, building up more and more charge until in her words, "I felt like I was going to burst." She would then climax at a different level of consciousness. I am not suggesting to eliminate orgasm, but rather to orgasm at a higher plateau of consciousness. This deepens the orgasm, as well as increases the overall feeling of connection to the partner as well as the world.

Concluding the Experience

When both you and your partner have completed, or feel finished and have gone through several plateaus, often it is nice to find a comfortable position to lie together. At this point the physical contact might be done without movement. Normally, while kissing, a partner's tongue is in your mouth moving against your tongue. Here, although the tongues are touching, there is actually no movement and attention is focused on the breath. This, can sometimes cause more energy to build. If it does, repeat the cycle again. If not, just *be*, keeping the attention on yourself as energy.

Please remember, this is a deep process that does not have the goal of orgasm. It is about experiencing a deeper connection to everything. By building up charge and reaching plateaus, you can experience both an interpersonal interconnection and a personal orgasm. Your purpose must be clear—that is the quantum approach.

Quantum Exercise 15

• ❖

Focus on the desire in the body as energy, rather than on the object of desire.

Step I: Either remember a time when you had a desire or notice a present-time desire.

Step II: Turn your attention away from the fantasy and notice where in your body you are experiencing this desire.

Step III: Notice the size and shape of the desire and the feelings associated with the desire.

Step IV: De-label the desire. Merge with and *Be* the desire as energy.

Step V: Feel your skin boundaries as being made of the same energy as the energy of desire.

Step VI: **Experience the air, the room, the floor, your chair, the rest of the universe including your thoughts as being made of the same energy.**

Step VII: **Make eye contact with other members of the group, seeing them as being made of the same energy as you.**

• •

The purpose of this exercise is the same as the others in this series, which is to move attention from the story, impressions, fantasy, or images to the delightful feelings as being made of energy. Simply put, take your attention and your energy, which is focused on the object of desire, and move it toward the feeling of desire itself and begin to view the desire as energy. Desires are often "put down" in many spiritual circles. Desires can, however, be seen in two ways; (1) Energy to be used or (2) a resistance to rejection or failure. In the later case when you feel a desire ask yourself; "By having this desire, what experience am I resisting." If you discover you are resisting a feeling such as rejection or failure, then use the earlier quantum exercises. In this way you can see the unwanted or resisted feelings as energy, and merge with them as energy with no resistance or intention.

• •

Practice

Format the rotating group facilitator might consider.

I'd like you to sit now for 5 to 10 minutes. Feel your body being physically supported, and focus on your breathing. Begin to develop a desire. Rather than seeing a small you on a screen, step into the person in your image so that you can see this fantasy from behind your own eyes rather than from a distance. From behind your own eyes, notice who you're with and what the situation

is. Notice if there are any sounds, if there is any particular smell or taste. Experience the sensations. Allow the
fantasy to get stronger and stronger and experience the
sensations, smells, tastes and sounds. Continue to allow
the experience to deepen.

Now, gently pull your attention away from the desire
and turn your attention into your own body and begin
to watch the desire, feelings and sensations inside your
body as you turn your attention toward the feelings and
sensations of desire. Witness the feelings and sensations
as energy. Focus your attention on the energy rather
than the fantasy.

Continue to watch those sensations as energy. Now
gently, feeling your body being pressed against the
floor, the chair or the couch, notice your body being
supported physically, and notice your breath. Very
gently, let your eyes open and come back to the room.

• •

At this time, it is good for the group facilitator to ask for
feedback. Recently at a workshop, a group member asked me,
"Why should I want to get rid of my desires?" I responded that many
Eastern spiritual disciplines suggest being desireless, but I do not.
My suggestion is, rather than chase after a desire and have the
fantasized desire in your mind, be in charge and be the one you're
running after. Notice that the pleasant sensations that are happening
in relation to your desire come from inside of you. Seeing the desire
and pleasant sensations as well as the image of what you are desiring
as energy, brings you back to yourself. This adds *choice* to the
experience. This works very well for people who are striving for
approval, recognition, and for work-aholics. Each believes, if they
get X, or have X, they will feel pleasant sensations. They are chasing
an image created by them. The quantum approach adds responsibility and choice.

Quantum Exercise 16

● ●

Food

Step I: Focus your attention on where in your body
            you experience the desire for food rather
            than on the fantasy of food.

Step II: Witness that desire as made of energy.

● ●

This exercise will plant a seed for you. The method for this
exercise is the same as the others. Let's imagine that you're sitting
at your desk at work, and all of a sudden you have the thought, "I
want a ham on rye" (or whatever your fantasy is). Your mind takes
off on that and you react to it. By the way, if you're fasting, or you
want to lose weight, you can use this exercise when you're hungry.
Focus on the hunger, on the desire for food, rather than on the food
and notice what happens.

I know for myself, and certainly with the clients I've worked
with, that food is an issue. Particularly under times of stress, we all
want to reach for something to stuff our face with, like chocolate.
One comedian I saw recently said, "Chocolate is the proof that God
exists." The method here is the same as all the previous exercises.
Focus on the sensations and feelings of hunger or the *desire* for
food, as made of energy. Once again, taking your attention away
from the food fantasy, you focus on the energy itself.

● ●

Practice 1

Format rotating group facilitator may consider.

**Allow a fantasy of food (chocolate, ice cream, etc.) to
come into your awareness. Notice where in your body**

you feel the desire or delightful sensations, i.e. your mouth, your stomach, etc. Next, witness these sensations as made of energy.

Practice 2

Format rotating group facilitator may consider.

Eyes closed. Take a small piece of chocolate or cake or whatever and place it in your mouth. Focus your attention on the sensations of delight, i.e., mouth watering, rather than the food itself. Keeping a small piece of food inside your mouth, experience the delightful sensations as energy.

• •

A student commented, "I've given up cigarettes, I've given up booze, and now I have to give up food?" "No," I told him, "I'm not saying that." The idea is to have a *choice*. Another student summed up his reactions with, "It feels like one of the real heavy problem areas." "Yes," I said, "it's much deeper than sex." You can live, although it's not much fun, without sex, but you cannot live without food. The purpose here is choice, and developing the ability to use all thoughts, feelings, emotions, and sensations as fuel to bring you back to a more clear, centered state.

Quantum Exercise 17

• •

Joy

Step I: *Find the source of your joy.*

I want to include this exercise because the mind fantasizes about joyful experiences. You can begin to find who you are in relation to them.

Practice

Format rotating group facilitator may consider:

Notice where and how you are sitting, and imagine a very joyful fantasy or experience. As it begins to develop, notice the delightful feelings inside you. Instead of watching a little you in the movie in your mind experiencing that joy, imagine unzipping the skin of that little person and stepping inside so that you are experiencing the joy. Go inside and find the space from which that joy arises. Find the source of that joy.

When you're ready, bring your awareness back, let your eyes open, and come back.

● ●

Here is a student comment: "When I went from the experience to the place inside, I found it in my heart; it was like light. I had trouble sustaining that. It would diminish, then expand, so I found that when I inhaled, I could control it and make it larger. It was as if I was playing with that, but I still couldn't sustain it."

I asked him, "Were you able to find the space beyond that?" "How do you get beyond that?" he asked. I replied, "You trace it back focusing on the witness of the breathing. Who is watching the joy? Your experience was that the joy comes and goes. You were trying to control it—that was also your experience. Who is witnessing not only the coming and going of joy but the attempt to control its coming and going?"

What is paramount is that we all focus on something "outside" ourselves as if, it were responsible for our internal experience. For example, in a psychotherapy context, often I will meet with people who are literally addicted to another person. In the literature, they are called "love addicts."

Now, in this situation, the other person is an object that the love addict believes is responsible for their experience. The love addict believes this so wholeheartedly, that the substance, i.e. person, is the only one that gives them these feelings.

A major step in the therapy process is to suggest that the

delightful sensations, which they label as love, are coming from inside of themselves; It's theirs. As with all the exercises in this section, we are asked to continually focus on the feelings as made of energy, not the object of feelings. By doing this, we own our experience as ours, a major turning point in owning our power. Normally, we give power to others, blame others, or give credit to another for our experience. This gives them the power because we think they are the source of our experience. The exercises move us to "getting" that our experience is ours.

Often times, we feel joyful internally, when our outer circumstances seem to dictate a different response. Also, at times we feel disappointed or down, when our external life might indicate we "should" feel an up. Sometimes clients I have seen actually feel their internal responses are inappropriate, as if there is some standard of what response is appropriate for a particular situation. These standards of response not only limit us but enable a deep sense of self-judgement or self-criticism. People sometimes label themselves or are labeled by others as "inappropriate," by some standard of society. When seeing responses as energy and observing them that way, this judgement is gone. We are able to feel what's there in our bodies.

> "Everyone can transform his impressions ... it is necessary to create a transforming agency at the point of intake of impressions ... this is the meaning of psychological transformation." (Nicoll, 1984:51-52)

Throughout all these exercises, we are asking for the transformation of psycho-emotional states. Gurdjieff suggests self-observation is the change agent. The change agent in Quantum Psychology, at this level, is observation and seeing the observed as energy. These exercises are designed to restore you as the source of your experience. Or, you might say, "these exercises are designed with your mind in mind."

Summary

As we leave the second level, it is important to reflect back on the path we traveled. In Level I, we explored the space between the thoughts as a wave function. In level I we also looked at the art of observing this wave function as it arose and subsided, into the space.

In Level II we are asked to see things in more of a quantum perspective, exploring the nature of our experience in terms of its energy aspect. What we noticed is that E-motions and feelings are made of energy, and that if you look at your body, you can feel the space they occupy.

One student said, "My anger was rectangular." I said to the group that she was seeing the shape and boundaries of the anger, and that by labeling the experience as anger she established boundaries. As she saw the anger as bounded energy, the boundaries became more diffused. What becomes important in understanding this is that the observer puts the label on the experience and, by doing that, contracts energy into a part-(icle). This part-(icle) has a solidness to it (mass), occupies a space, and exists in time, as David Bohm has stated.

In Chapter III, we talked about the observer, and in this chapter, the energy function. In the next chapter "Getting to Zero" we will look at the mass function and how when energy is contracted and labeled, it is experienced as a part-(icle) losing its connection to the whole, with mass and size. In the next chapter we discover how the act of labeling solidifies energy into a part-(icle) and how that part-(icle) became diffused and transmutes itself when the label is taken off.

Why do I emphasize the word "part-(icle)"? Because when we label undifferentiated energy, we make it a *part*, separate from the whole, hence part-(icle). In the next chapter, we will look at how not only to own our power or energy, but also how we create our experience of that energy. This will bring us to Werner Heisenberg's Uncertainty Principle, "that reality is observer created," and in terms of Quantum Psychology, how we create our own experience and interpretation of *subjective* reality.

FIVE

GETTING TO ZERO

Zero grants existence permission to be.

Tarthang Tulku
Knowledge of Time and Space

If the preparation of the measurement is modified, the properties of the particle will change.

Fritjof Capra
Tao of Physics

Probably one of the most exciting and *provocative* theories in quantum physics is Werner Heisenberg's Uncertainty Principle. Heisenberg in the mid-1920s was able to demonstrate that the observer, by the choices he/she made, influenced the outcome of a physics experiment. For the first time, we as observers of life were seen as inseparable from life. The observer not only viewed a world "out there," as Newtonian physics had claimed, but it altered, influenced, and some physicists would claim, created, what it saw through the act of observation.

> "What is *out there* apparently depends, in a rigorous mathematical sense, as well as a philosophical one, upon what we decide *in here*. The new physics tells us that an observer cannot observe without altering what he sees." (Zukav, 1984:185)

Level 3

The observer is the creator of the part-(icle)/mass aspect of the universe.

This theory becomes a major "quantum jump," that Quantum Psychology develops to help understand human problem states.

Principle: The observer, through the act of observation, creates, his/her subjective internal response pattern, i.e. their experience.

> "This means that how we subjectively experience events, interactions, and our inner self is observer-created ... created by us. This reality suggests a further one: that we, as the observers of our experience, choose *how* an experience is experienced. For example, if I say "I like you," you might create any number of responses: (1) "That's nice," (2) "They really didn't mean it," (3) "If he only knew what I was really like, he'd never feel that way," (4) "I wonder what he really wants from me." (Wolinsky, 1991:2-3)

This principle guides us through Chapter V. Noted physicist Fred Wolf speculates, "How could there be a mechanical universe out there, if the universe changed (in here) every time we alter how we observe it?"

Because of the active influence exerted by the observer, quantum theorist John Wheeler has added a significant refinement by changing the word observer to the word *participator.*

"Zero point" is a term we utilize which includes the observer plus the ability the observer has to create and construct subjective reality through the act of observation. Zero point can therefore be called the point outside of consciousness which observes and therefore creates and constructs the subjective experience of reality.

In the early 1930s, the now-famous Copenhagen Debates took place in an attempt to hash-out the nature of reality according to the newly developed quantum physics. This nature of perceived, subjective realities is central in our exploration of "zero point".

> "The Copenhagen interpretation properly consists of two distinct parts: (1) There is no reality in the absence of observation; (2) Observation creates reality. "You create your own reality," is the theme of Fred Wolf's *Taking the Quantum Leap.*" (Herbert, 1985:17).

In this chapter we will focus on the second part, "observation creates reality". In Chapter IX and X, we will focus on the first part, "There is no reality in the absence of observation."

The exploration of zero point is a pivotal juncture in looking at how we continually create our subjective experience of reality. To understand and dismantle our own personal aspect of "observer created" reality is the theme of this chapter.

The realities we interpret as objective, we can begin to see are, in actuality, subjective. Our very act of observing, as stated in the Cophenhagen interpretation, creates our realities. To shift awareness to this level of consciousness is the focus of this zero point chapter and exercises. The point of observation here, is called "zero point". Often in workshops, I ask participants to "create an image of a deer in the middle of the room." Then I ask them to take their attention (observation) off of it and let it disappear—it does—then to look to see if it is still there. It reappears. Why? Because the act of observation creates the observed. In this case, the act of observation again creates the image of the deer.

Quantum Exercise 18

● ●

Observation creates reality.

Step I	**Create an image of a deer in the middle of your room.**
Step II	**Stop observing it and allow it to disappear.**
Step III:	**Check to see if it is still there.**

● ●

Generally, it re-creates itself through the act of you looking for it. Sometimes workshop participants cannot "get rid of the deer." Why? Because they keep looking to see if it's gone. The looking creates the imaginary deer's presence. This phenomenon also occurs in our personal psychology. We create, through the use of attention, a particular subject (thought, etc.) and observe it appearing. It also disappears as we take our attention away.

Exploring the "Creative Aspect of the Observer"

This section, like the last series integrates Eastern philosophy, psychology and quantum physics. These areas will be explored from theoretical and experiential modalities. This will enable the reader to experience the "creative aspect of the observer." We will entertain the notion of getting back to who we are by de-constructing various old created parts within our perceptions that are no longer of any value.

For example, the observer, through observation, can create the subjective experience of hopelessness. Unfortunately, as will be demonstrated later, the observer fuses with, and experientially becomes, this hopelessness and thinks that is who he/she is. A teacher in India once said, "Personality is a mis-taken identity." As we become identified with these created aspects, we conclude this is who we are, rather than this is what I constructed to perceive myself. Another way to say it is this is a *self lens* that I created, and it will define me and my world.

Practice Realities, an Inner Exploration

Let us first start with physics as our point of departure. In physics there is a central question which concerns the nature of matter. This question is relative to the experiment and to the observer of the experiment which is crucial. The question that remains, "Is the nature of matter a wave or a particle?" We will explore the varying nature of particles and how this impacts internal, subjective realities.

In the last two chapters, we explored the wave-like function of internal reality and its energy function. In this chapter we will focus on the part-(icle) and mass function of reality, how aspects or parts of ourself were created by us at an early age by the observer, and now act as automatic behaviors, and *self lens*.

In psychology, the term "part" refers to an aspect of our individual personality. Using this terminology and combining it with quantum physics, helps introduce the concept of the part-(icle). A part-(icle) is part of the "unbroken wholeness of the Quantum world." Like a part of a person, a part-(icle) is a part of the whole. Furthermore, when the whole or the undifferentiated energy presented in our last chapter is broken down through labeling, the whole becomes a solid mass-like structure called a part-(icle), in this case a part of our personality. Once we identify with a part, we become limited and cut-off from the whole, feeling heavy, solid and massive. We lose the lightness we seek due to the rigidity of boundaries and the process of fusion and identification.

In the following exploration of consciousness, we will view our inner world in the context of the nature of mass and part-(icles). In earlier exercises we were asked to observe thoughts that come and go, and feelings that come and go. We have explored witnessing from a nonjudgmental observer place, where the phenomena of these transient states floating by are perceived. We have also noticed that all of the above have a particular energy, which is transmutable and transformable as exemplified in the practice of seeing particular emotions, thoughts, or body sensations as energy. Now we can begin to explore how beliefs and experiences can be viewed as part-(icles). The following exercise continues our building block approach in understanding how reality is created by our subjective observation and creation of automatic responses.

Quantum Exercise 19

• •

Labels create part-(icles)

Step I: Notice an emotion that has troubled you, i.e. sadness, anger, hurt.

Step II: Decide the emotion is "bad or unwanted". Notice how your inner experience feels.

Step III: De-label it, and see it as energy and *observe*.

• •

Usually people notice that their labels filter and influence how they experience an emotion. How we chose to label an emotion or thought, influences our internal, subjective experience. A former decision about an experience, a former belief about the world, prevents us from allowing in new information. Hence, through our label, we experience and condense an emotion into a part-(icle), which is condensed energy. Due to the fixed nature of our thoughts or beliefs, the condensed energy, which has become a part-(icle), begins to become more dense energy or mass. (See illustration # 6 &7)

The more it is reinforced through labeling and reinforcing experiences, the more fixed in consciousness the part-(icle) becomes. The energy becomes more solidified since the person holds a set of fixed beliefs around it. Different or new information cannot flow in or out. (See illustration # 8). Consciousness then becomes

Illustration 6

This is undifferentiated energy before the label of fear is fixed.

Illustration 7

Below is what occurs when undifferentiated energy is labeled fear. The energy becomes a solid particle with mass.

Illustration 8

Below we see solidified energy, solid with mass and boundaries. Here, an individual is saying, "I like you," but the boundaried energy, labeled fear, cannot allow it inside. Simply put, once energy is labeled and made into a particle or mass—nothing can get in and nothing can get out.

less fluid for the person; they experience their choices as less spacious and more condensed and heavy (mass). They may even lose the ability to perceive the part-(icle) as a belief. Instead they begin to see themselves as a particular belief, with little choice over their experience. In a nutshell the observer fuses with and becomes his/her beliefs, forgetting he/she is the observer, labeler and creator of the neutral energy. This is done through the process of decision. Noted Buddhist teacher Tarthang Tulku says it this way:

> "In each act of positioned knowing, there is a 'point of decision,' a vital 'zero point,' 'before' knowing is accomplished." (Tulku, 1990:270).

Here, Tarthang Tulku is suggesting that zero point is before knowing and fusing with what is known. Zero point, in Quantum Psychology is the knower and observer and exists at this level *before* the known. In quantum physics terms, the knower, through the act of observation, creates what is known. In psychological terms, the observer creates his/her experience through the creative act of observation. Notice how Buddhism, psychology and physics overlap in Quantum Psychology to help understand how subjective reality is constructed.

Once the observer creates and fuses with a thought, he/she loses the ability to see that the part-(icle) belief has a boundary. Rather, through identification with the labeled energy, the observer feels boundaried, contracted and limited by his/her own created reality. This experience is merely an extension of the self-created belief system.

We will explore next how to work with these perceived part-(icles) on emotional and belief levels, and learn to identify boundaried experiences versus spacious non-boundaried experiences, the latter of which are more like the subatomic world of quantum physics. We do acknowledge the boundaried world, but do choose to explore the spaciousness of non-boundaried existence to create a larger context in which to experience ourselves.

When we look at our own experience, we can notice that when we *believe* something is true, we *feel* it is true, and it becomes subjectively true for us. Then, events in the world that seemingly *happen* to us are interpreted and funneled through that belief system. This reinforces the standard we have of the world and ourselves. By judging our experience as good, bad, or neutral we begin to solidify our own perceived realities. The more we continue to access these realities and label them, we create more density and mass in our thoughts and emotional patterns. Thus, the energy becomes less fluid and more dense. This occurs in our subjective perception, not in external reality. As David Bohm has suggested, "everything interpenetrates everything else." In order to function in the world, we categorize our experience, which breaks up the liquid nature of consciousness. We believe the reality we create is the *true* one. As this energy continues to be labeled, the belief in our internal reality and its *perceived* nature solidifies.

An old friend of mine once said, "Stephen, I feel you are this way." I said, "I'm not." She said, "But I *feel* you are." She had labeled me this particular way, and would and could not see beyond her label. In cognitive therapy this is called "emotional reasoning."

"At the root of this distortion is the belief that what you feel must be true. If you feel like a loser, then you must be a loser." (Davis, 1981:22).

Here, my friend is labeling me and feeling her label; this denies any new or other information from getting in, unless she can let go of the label. I'm sure we can all identify with being labeled by another to be a certain way, even if it's not true. How often have all of us spent time really trying to explain we are different from the way we are being labeled and perceived, only to be left frustrated, feeling alienated, isolated and misunderstood.

Quantum Exercise 20

• •

Step I: Observe a belief. Pick beliefs about yourself and notice them floating by.

Step II: See them as solidified part-(icles) of energy.

Step III: Practice stepping into and merging with the part-(icle); notice how your experience changes. The world generally seems denser and more constricted when there is a fixed belief about your world. We feel heavier.

Step IV: Step out of the belief or part-(icle) and observe. Notice the alteration of your experience, perhaps a feeling of lightness, non-attachment, or spaciousness. Also notice this in the everyday world when you interact with someone with fixed beliefs, or when intense emotional states occur. Your energy or spaciousness has a heavier density. When observing the part-(icle), there will be more lightness or space. (Chapter VII on space will discuss this further.)

• •

To further understand, let's look at the same process from a quantum viewpoint.

Quantum Exercise 21

• •

See the energy of a belief called "nobody loves me," with boundaries. See how the energy solidifies as you label the experience, and it develops a part-(icle)-like and heavy, dense, mass-like structure. Follow these steps to have a more grounded understanding through this exercise.

Step I: Look at the energy again without judgement.

Step II: Perceive a part-(icle) you believe or label like "nobody loves me." Intentionally label or believe it.

Step III: Notice that when you believe it, you identify or fuse with it and feel less spacious.

Step IV: Now, step out of the part-(icle) and see how your experience becomes more spacious, when you see it as energy. (See illustration #9).

Notice as you label and separate the energy into a particular belief, there is less space. When you identify with the part-(icle), and experience yourself believing it, it becomes you. Your experience then is, "I am unlovable."

• •

The consequences of solidifying energy into a belief are feeling heavier, denser, and also believing it as true. Hence, even if a partner

Illustration 9

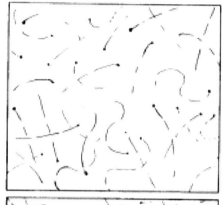

STEP I:
UNDIFFERENTIATED
ENERGY

STEP II:
LABELED AS
"NOBODY
LOVES ME"

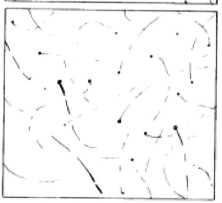

STEP III:
DE-LABELED
AND JUST SEEN
AS ENERGY

is offering love, that energy cannot be taken in because the prior created part-(icle) will not allow it. It remains a block to the present reality or energy being offered. The part-(icle) now has boundaries which are self-imposed and believed. That part-(icle) becomes your experience of reality.

Regaining Choice
Over Our Experience

Our purpose in presenting zero point philosophy and techniques is to allow people to have more choice over their beliefs and experience. In order for this to occur, old beliefs need to be looked at, and de-constructed. This allows for more space in consciousness. As this occurs, people become aware that there is an observer who is the creative source of beliefs, who determines how experiences are interpreted or labeled. At this juncture we do *not* employ a new belief system but rather allow the person to experience the observer as the creative source of experience. In order to "get to zero," the observer/creator must de-label and de-construct prior created reality.

Why would someone want to get to zero? Because at zero you can just *be* and connect with people without the filters, beliefs, and obstacles that keep popping up in our consciousness. These old "pop-ups" (inner voices, old pictures and associations), prevent us from just being in present time and connecting at a being to being level, rather than through prior created structures.

You might say that in most of our relationships we connect through our roles. We often feel lonely and alienated because all our stuff gets in the way. Zero point allows us to connect being to being. At that level, there is no loneliness, no alienation.

To re-state, Tarthang Tulku,

"By standing in contrast to what is, *Zero* grants existence permission to be." (Tulku, 1990:271)

Therefore, beliefs and experiences must be examined. Other systems have presented theories regarding this issue. There are opposing views in regard to the creation of beliefs and experience.

Many people believe you first have an experience, and then you organize a belief to fit the experience.

For example, if a father is repeatedly abusive to a child, the child could decide and "globalize" * that "all men are mean." Based on the child's interpretation of reality, this could begin to actualize in all his/her relationships with men. Dr. Eric Berne, the creator of transactional analysis in the 1960s and author of the book *Games People Play* explored this territory. He summarized that beliefs were created during particular experiences, and that these "games," as he labeled them, became automatic strategies that people would use to relate to others. A child that is victimized decides he has no choice but to act like a victim to survive in his family. His father could be the persecutor, his mother the rescuer. Since the family has agreed, on some level, to play this game out, it is mutually reinforced and internalized by the child.

Then, as he goes further into the world, he sees himself as an eternal victim. This game becomes the only way he feels like he will be taken care of, or be cared about. His perception of caring and love become automatic from repeated experiences—automatically he believes he is a victim and interprets everything through that filter. He literally has tunnel vision. Since the only way he received attention from his parents was to remain a victim, he continues this and projects this automatic strategy. This belief structure is so reinforced it influences him to continue this relationship with other people. He begins to *look* for a rescuer or persecutor. Different beliefs and patterns become part-(icles) in his consciousness. People tend to be attracted to each other in terms of opposites or trade-offs. The victim, who longs to be taken care of, becomes involved with a person, who needs to take care of, like a rescuer. In consciousness, the part-(icles) become identified and frozen. People no longer feel like the creators of their lives and choices.

In terms of understanding human psychological dynamics from a quantum perspective, our ordinary outlook must be framed differently. In quantum terms, the observer of the experience influences how the experience is interpreted through the act of observation. *Subjective* reality becomes filtered† and colored by the process of being observer-created. Hence, the reality becomes

---

*Globalize is a term used in Cognitive Therapy when we create a belief and make it a global truth.

†Filtering is another term used in cognitive therapy to describe how we "take in" some experiences and "filter out others."

labeled by the observer, and the nature of the experience is decided. For example, if Dad treated you in a particular manner, the observer creates the meaning or the way the experience is construed. One person may decide abuse is love, another may decide abuse is not happening, and another may decide abuse hurts; all realities are given a meaning, which condenses energy into part-(icles). In this decision process, the observer freezes or holds energy in a particular way. This condensation of energy then becomes more rigid because it is held in place by particular beliefs, attitudes, perceptions.

Observers, as they label experiences, tend to identify and fuse with them. They decide, "This is me." From this point their energy becomes more bound by belief and, as we have demonstrated, an observer-created reality. This process is experienced in individual consciousness as a "part-(icle)"—it has psychic weight, mass, and energy of its own. This is why in therapy the therapist refers to a part of you being this way or that way. When people become a part-(icle), they no longer experience the space or choice to see life differently. The tension held in these part-(icles) remains and the observer function colors the experience from its own filtering. The true nature of observation, or the witness, is lost.

Unfortunately, as we become fused* with the part-(icle), we lose the ability to have choice over our reality. The perspective of life becomes narrow and "stuck." Many forms of therapy and spiritual practice are cognizant of witnessing, being mindful, or awake. They ask that we look at the particular patterns. In this way we begin to observe our limitation, but do not find ourselves out of these individual part-(icle) realities. It is important to clarify and reinforce: we do not create Dad to be a certain way, but we create our *subjective* experience of Dad being a certain way.

This is our departure point. Most Eastern and Western approaches ask us to be aware of, watch, notice, observe, or witness, "our process." The problem is the same one I experienced meditating three to five hours a day for 12 years. I could witness and observe everything. The problem was that I was witnessing the same "stuff" over and over again, whether there was just a blank space or an unpleasant thought or feeling. What it took me twelve years to realize was that the observer creates that which he/she is observing. This instantaneous process of observer creating his/her object, and

---

* Fusion is a term developed in structural family therapy.

giving the appearance that the object was always there, left me stuck. I experienced this phenomenon because I, as the observer, was creating through the act of observation, an internal experience. The next quantum jump, takes us out of the illusion of passive observer of the world to the observer-created reality. This is where witnessing as a meditation practice must be left behind, or like the experience presented, you will be witnessing and observing the mind forever, since you as the observer are creating the mind to observe. Gestalt psychology, so aware of unfinished business which keeps popping up as foreground, calls zero point, "the point where you (the observer) meet the now."

The Approach

The next approach allows individuals to see that the observer creates what it observes, in terms of how an experience is subjectively experienced. Without an approach or "how to," it would be just more mental masturbation. Here the proof is in the pudding. If you can, as the observer, *stop* creating subjective reality, then the approach works. Otherwise, it is just more ideas for the mind.

Here the active observer of quantum physics, meets the more passive Eastern observer/witness. We do not create an unpleasant incident happening to us—car accident, war, loss of a loved one. However, as we discovered in exploring part-(icle) realities, we do funnel our experience and judge and categorize it according to our constructed belief systems. In this way we influence how an experience is subjectively experienced.

Perhaps a child has progressed through a difficult life: poverty, abuse and pain. He/she could easily choose a global belief such as, "Life is hard." As the observer decides this reality, then the reality is *subjectively* created again and again. The present-time reality becomes fixed by the observer/creator, and all experiences are interpreted this way. Thus, a person's present experience is clouded by the past created filters. These realities were subjective at the time but also based on the external reality presented by the person. However functional in the past, it becomes dysfunctional when created automatically because the person loses choice.

The point to start exploring this phenomenon is with the subjective reality you are creating *automatically*. In this level, the observer, which is you, is asked to learn the skill of creating knowingly instead of unknowingly. This skill involves the ability to cease or stop creating a subjective experience. This new-found ability takes us from the victim position, of feeling unaware and helpless about our experience, to being able to choose or cease a certain automatic subjective reality.

Our next section provides a context and experiential exercises to help us take responsibility for our personal, subjective reality. The goal is to free the observer so he/she may be unobstructed from prior created realities and experiences. Here, an observer can observe without the distractions that pop-up in the mind.

Exploring the Creation of our Realities

Philosophies look at creation of experience in many ways; zero point process presents the principle that subjective and internal experiences of reality are observer created. We choose to see, feel, and label experiences according to our "subjective lens." Removing the subjective lens allows us to begin the process of seeing through our quantum lens. Each of us will determine various subjective responses according to the reality we chose. Obviously we do not create the physical manifestation of the world, such as the car in the driveway. Instead we do create our reactions to physical reality. We all have many responses which pop-up when we observe a scene, person, or object. If someone looks at a red car, his/her creation may be, in a subjective sense, "I like red cars; they're sexy," or "I don't like red cars; policeman give them to many tickets." All these responses allow the observer to influence the internal-subjective responses.

This principle operates in quantum physics and also in our internal, psychological response system. One of the goals of the zero point process is to begin to clear away our automatic observer-created labels. This transcends the subjective reality we hold in place by our prior conditioning. We begin to clear out and allow the space in our consciousness that brings us back to "zero" ... just pure observation.

We then have the opportunity to view reality without prior thoughts, feelings, emotions, associations, or body responses, which influence our experience in the moment. In other words, we have the opportunity to view reality "Without any stuff going on." Our old filters are usually prior responses, which were created and left in a holding pattern and continue to impact our subjective experience. We become unable to chose a free or unfettered moment in the present.

An example could be a traumatic incident, such as, a child witnessing the death of his mother in an accident with a red car. Because of the prior experience of horror, pain, grief, shock, and abandonment, which became associations, all red cars have stigmas attached to them. The emotional responses of collapse, crying, feeling intense loss, stopping breathing, etc., also become linked to this shattering trauma. This complete Gestalt becomes fused with red cars. No longer is this person free to see a red car without some internal, prior response and creation. Every time a red car goes by, there is an odd feeling, avoidance, or memory, that passes through consciousness because all red cars are linked to this over-whelming loss. Even years later, shopping, driving, or being a passenger in a red car evolves into a situation possibly to avoid or dislike intensely.

The past observer-created reactions are carried into the present; they have not been released. This individual becomes *fused* with the associations, feelings, decisions that appear forever linked with the trauma. Red cars are never experienced in a free, open way. Instead they are weighted in experience and consciousness with this past collection of unresolved creations.

In relationships, often we are weighted down by past abandon-ments, betrayals. This, in our present-time relationship keeps us distanced and guarded. In essence, we are taking past upsets and projecting them into the present and future. Therefore, we stay closed in treating past-time relationships as though they occur in present time.

Principle: Once the observer decides a reality is true, there is a tendency to maintain that reality by automatically creating it repeat-edly.

The ability to choose becomes lost in this rigid boundary, which can influence the present, although the person remains unaware of this prior decision. Once, when a women was participating in therapy, she remembered an incident that had been traumatic for her as young child. She had discovered her parents making love in the shower. Her father yelled at her and she was frozen with fear, terror, and confusion. Her attention became fixed on a toothbrush; this helped absorb her attention away from the painful experience. The observer of her experience labeled the trauma as fearful, and her bodily response and psychological response became one of intense fear. Years later, as an adult, when she wished to make love with her husband the automatic fear response, which manifested in a feeling of frozenness, kept manifesting. The old response was again re-created from the automatic response of the observer-created reality. Somehow, every time she saw a tooth-brush in the bathroom, unknowingly the past association operated and she would feel a "sense" of fear.

Quantum Exercise 22

• •

Step I: **Remember an automatic response that re-occurs in your life.**

Step II: **Watch the response.**

Step III: **Notice the automatic feelings, associations, emotions, body responses that seem to "happen to you," automatically. This is the experience that occurs when automatic observer created realities continue to generate.**

Step IV: **Observe and intentionally create the thought, feeling or memory. Make a xerox copy of the thought, feeling, or memory.**

Step V: **See the "pop-up" (thought, feeling or memory) as energy.**

• •

Many therapies put emphasis on what occurred in childhood. Look instead at how the incident becomes time frozen and held in place by the observer. The observer, who is not time bound and linear, creates this experience in time. Time appears to anchor it. The frozen incident seems like it is always present. Instead the observer continues to create it, and the reactions to it and around it, or in response to it. The principle follows that the observer creates the *subjective internal* experience, not the actual event, and then the observer pretends not to have create the internal experience.

For example, many times you might be walking along or chatting with a friend, and anger or sadness, or a sudden "uncomfortable" feeling might emerge inside of you. "Where did this come from?" you ask yourself. "Why am I feeling this way?" The appearance is that the feeling "happened" to you. The observer re-creates the experience and then pretended not to, as if he/she (the observer) had nothing to do with it.

Another example could be having a difference of opinion with your spouse. One part of you responds with hurt, the other with anger. Each feels the emotion just happened to them; instead each had something to do with it. One friend of mine used to say, "I realized that no matter what happened to me in my life good or bad that there was always the same person there—me, (the observer). I realized that I must have had something to do with it."

Instead of asking, "Where is this anger coming from?" look at the creation of the emotion, attitude, belief. Generally, we have evolved through therapy, spiritual practice, or the general hard knocks of life, into allowing and accepting our feelings. The most important thing I got from years of therapy was it was okay to feel what I was feeling and to be where I was. The next step is to "grok " (get) that we are responsible for and created and constructed these beliefs that yield feelings. We do this knowingly or unknowingly through the act of observation.*

Conflicting Beliefs

If we become absorbed in creating our subjective realities, our responses to particular situations, why are new realities or internal

---

*This process of labeling is discussed by Dr. Albert Ellis, the founder of Cognitive Therapy.

programs so difficult to change? Many proponents of new age therapies attempt to alter consciousness, as do proponents of education or hypnosis. They present the hypothesis that we can create new ways of being through visualization, the power of positive thinking, meditations, self-hypnosis, affirmations, or the act of the *unconscious mind*. These methods often suggest we disallow negative associations or thoughts through affirmation or reassociation. Two important pieces are missed in these processes.

Principle: One cannot maintain a new reality against the existing, prior-created reality.

This practice sets up an increased resistance to change. The realities become oppositional. An example would be attempting to believe a new reality of "life is easy." Unfortunately, the old creation or belief of "life is hard" still exists in consciousness. One creation cannot be *overcome* by another. A positive thought, decision, or reassociation does not have more mass or power to override a negative thought, decision, reassociation or creation. The existing thought must be dealt with because it was created first and remains in consciousness.

Principle: The first belief that is created becomes a person's point of reference and therefore carries the most power. It becomes the person's standard to measure experience.

Hence, the reference point of the original belief, "Life is hard," becomes the initial point of reference. And, it will remain so until the observer can understand, first, that he/she exists prior to his/her belief, and second, that he/she chose the belief that has become the filtering system for incoming and outgoing perceptions and experiences. Once an observer "gets" this, experientially, he/she can, in present time, stop creating this filtering system or belief called "Life is hard."

A classic example to which we can all relate is feeling inadequate or not smart (the first created part-(icle) made through decision). Next, we try to over-compensate, working very hard to prove we are *not* inadequate (Second part-(icle) creation). Notice that no matter how much we prove or try to prove our adequacy, we continually feel the first creation or inadequacy. Even if we achieve success, we are always comparing the feeling to our feeling of inadequacy. In essence, the inadequate feelings become our *reference point*!!!

> "Our whole reality is constructed by constantly making such comparisons. Our senses, which describe our reality to us, are making these comparisons all the time. Unfortunately, our senses, having no absolute reference line, must generate their own relative reference line. But whenever we perceive something, we always perceive differences only, whether it be heat or cold, light or darkness, quiet or noisy, always compared to relative quantities. We have no absolute measure of anything, so far as our daily reality is concerned (Bentov, 1977:22)

A client I worked with in therapy, an adolescent, felt inadequate in comparison to her older sister, who because of her age always seemed to do everything better and more successfully. My client came up short whenever she tried to achieve anything on her own. She perpetually began to compare herself to the "standard" of her older sister and was unable to be herself. She had fused with her sister, who had become her internal standard. Whenever she attempted a new way of being, she would automatically compare herself with the sister and feel the old emotions of inadequacy, failure and confusion. Her belief, "I want to be an adequate person" was continually compared with the sister, who was adequate. Simply put, the observer took a picture of the sister and held it in consciousness with her feelings of being inadequate in comparison to her. This is the first creation. She then creates an overcompensating part-(icle) to prove she's not inadequate. By trying to negate the first creation, and by resisting it, we set up a dichotomy. The observer sees the old pictures, associations, memories, and is unable to choose a new step into a freer consciousness because the previous creations are what we make our choices from instead of a clear, open space. Often we hold old pictures there as a way to resist being like them. It takes energy and effort to continually hold the picture in place and resist being like it, while, at the same time, hoping to evolve a different reality. For example, if a person decides, "I don't want to be like mom, she must always hold a picture of mom in her consciousness, (first creation) so she knows what not to be (second creation). This means, since the first creation is strongest she becomes mom and resists being like mom in a constant internal struggle.

Quantum Exercise 23

● ●

Step I: See two standards or part-(icles) in space. (For example, one part-(icle) is the belief "I want to be like my sister," the other part-(icle) could be," I want to be myself, not like my sister."

Step II: Merge with one part-(icle) and experience this reality.

Step III: Merge into the other part-(icle) and experience this reality.

Step IV: Step in between the two conflicting parts and experience the emotion between the two part-(icles).

Step V: Feel this emotion and conflict (energy) that maintains them in place.

Step VI: Now observe the two part-(icles) as made of the same energy.

Step VII: Notice what occurs.

● ●

When we attempt to resist the first part-(icle) or creation we continue to re-enforce it. This occurs in thought affirmation when the original belief or part-(icle) has not been seen as made of the same energy as the second part-(icle). An affirmation, "Life is easy," usually is resisting the prior belief, "Life is hard." To continue to insist life is easy basically supports or continues to be linked to the old belief that life is hard. The two conflicting beliefs are connected. Often in therapy there is an attempt to "get rid" of the *life is hard* and keep *life is easy*. These two constructs are totally connected so that *life is easy* creates back *life is hard* and *life is hard* creates back *life is easy*. Both part-(icles) need to be seen as made of the same substance—energy.

We generally would not insist on a new belief or affirmation unless we were still linked or believed the prior creation. So as we write, "I am worthy of making money," we are actually supporting the old maxim, "I'm unworthy of making money." Each time we write, "I am worthy of making money," we are re-enforcing its opposite, earlier-created belief.

The important point is to be able to appreciate that an observer constructed thoughts in the mind and placed them on automatic. In my former book, *Trances People Live: Healing Approaches in Quantum Psychology*, the observer creates a response to an event. If the response, which I called a "trance", works, then the observer places the response (trance) on automatic. Why is it called a trance? Because the observer shrinks himself/herself down into a smaller part-(icle) and experiences life through or from that part-(icle), or filter. The observer, by doing this, restricts his/her vision and sees the world with tunnel vision. *(See Illustration #10)*

The principle explored here is "the observer has no preference." Getting back to zero allows people to view the world without automatic preferences. A preference comes from a part-(icle) I-dentity not from the observer. We all may choose to like a particular food, relationship, color, but the experience is much different when this choice occurs with no preference or outcome, rather than from old, learned associations in the mind.

The zero point process allows the observer to view what occurs in the mind, rather than attaching, identifying or *preferring*. This allows us to step outside the arena of the part-(icle) and release prior thoughts, associations, emotions, and sensations. This puts us in present time. These are the components which normally keep us from remaining in the observer state.

The question often arises in workshops, "Isn't this like meditation?"

Illustration 10

Notice how an observer can see the world with no obstruction if there is no part-(icle) blocking the view. On the contrary, if the world is viewed from a part-(icle) rather than from the observer, the "world view" is limited.

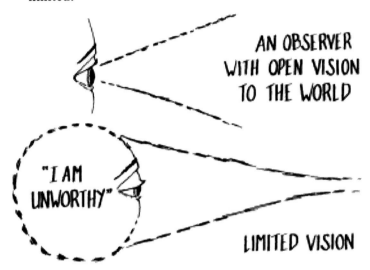

AN OBSERVER
WITH OPEN VISION
TO THE WORLD

"I AM
UNWORTHY"

LIMITED VISION

"Meditation (dhynana) is an unbroken flow of thought toward the object of concentration. In other words, meditation is prolonged concentration.... The process of meditation is often compared to the pouring of oil from one vessel to another, in a steady, unbroken stream." (Isherwood, 1953:122)

This suggests, that meditation requires the efforts of focusing and concentrating. It is hoped this focusing, like placing a magnifying glass in sunlight and focusing the heat from the sun in a single ray, focuses enough energy to burn a leaf. In the same way, focusing and concentrating will burn the leaf part-(icle). The problem is there is no responsibility nor acknowledgment that, the *one who is concentrating (the observer)* put the leaf or part-(icle) there in the first place. Meditation is the skill of concentration and brings about many benefits, *but* in order to go beyond part-(icle) realities, an observer must take responsibility for putting the observed reality there in the first place, so the observer can stop putting the beliefs part-(icle) there.

East Meets West

This is where Eastern meditation and physics again join hands with Western psychotherapy. Western psychotherapy asks clients to acknowledge and take responsibility for their experience. In other words, a client constructs his/her subjective experience. Psychology offers *awareness* of a created pattern. It tries to interpret it, or work through some "old unfinished business," so the pattern is not repeated again. In Eastern meditation and Sufi traditions, we are asked to observe, or just witness the mind, or to *concentrate*. We are asked to become so absorbed that the nature of the object will shine forth; this absorption is termed "samadhi." Quantum physics, on the other hand, suggests that through the act of observation, *we create what we observe*. This is "zero point."

Tradition	Approach
Sufi and Eastern meditation	Observation
Psychotherapy	Take responsibility and acknowledge created reality
Quantum physics	Observer creates subjective, observed experience

Quantum Psychology asks the practitioner (1) to observe (Sufi and Eastern traditions), (2) take responsibility and experience subjective reality (Western psychotherapy), and (3) realize the observer is creating through the act of observation its subjective thoughts, feelings, etc. (quantum physics).

Quantum Exercise 24

• •

Experiencing the boundary and shape of a thought, belief or emotion.

Step I: First allow yourself to chose a feeling you are experiencing.

Step II: Intentionally observe the feeling.

Step III: Intentionally merge with and experience it.

Step IV: Notice the size and shape of the feeling.

Step V: Be the feeling inside the shape.

Step VI: Step out of the shape and notice how your experience changes.

• •

The shapes and boundaries create the illusion of separateness. These boundaries allow us to identify and be in varying emotional, intellectual experiences that without contracted boundaries would not occur. (A person would only experience one undifferentiated energy!) Everything would flow into everything else, or as Bohm recounts, "Everything interpenetrates everything else." Other disciplines have acknowledged the importance of the boundary and how each part-(icle) has its own shape. Jung asked that the energy be seen as a shape. Esoteric literature calls it a "thoughtform;" quantum physics, "part-(icles)." Psychology calls it "parts" or "patterns." In Sanskrit, eastern religions call these compacted thoughtforms "samskaras".

> "Thought has a *definite form*…the thought becomes for a time a living creature you called a thought-force." (Besart, 1969)

As noted in the above exercise, we can see that thoughts, emotions, sensations, and body responses have boundaries or shapes. By observing these thoughtforms, elaborated on by well-known psychic Edgar Cayce you can begin to notice that you do not have to be identified as being these thoughtforms. Noted physicist John Wheeler calls these thoughtforms "bubbles in a pond" or "quantum foam". Each of these bubbles, part-(icles), contains feelings, thoughts, emotions, associations—but also emptiness. Usually, this is the "space" we do not acknowledge because we are so identified with the other material. As observation witnessing occurs, we begin to be less pulled, or identified, with these bubbles and become more aware of the space. At first, they appear to be more bubbles, thoughtforms, or part-(icles); but, as we create them intentionally we experience more space. Edgar Cayce defined us as many clusters of these thoughtforms. It is interesting to note that all these clusters hold stories, memories, ideas, and history.

Quantum Exercise 25

• •

Step I: First allow yourself to choose a feeling you are experiencing.

Step II: Intentionally observe the feeling.

Step III: Notice the size and shape of the feeling.

Step IV: Fuse with the feeling and experience inside the shape. Notice how you experience the shape. How is it different than observing the emotion?

Step V: Step out of it, and notice how your experience changes.

Step VI: See the part-(icle) or thoughtform as made of energy.

Step VII: **Realize that it is just a bubble or part-(icle) you created through the act of labeling the energy.**

Step VIII: See it as energy and allow the part-(icle) to do whatever it does.

• •

Acknowledging the creative aspect of the observer allows us to de-label and, therefore, stop creating, unknowingly, thoughts and feelings out of energy. We forget that how we define ourselves has been constructed by us (the observer/creator). The problem is that the boundaries or edges of these forms become lost when we become fused or merged with them. Only as we observe these created realities with some objectivity do we begin to notice they have shapes and boundaries. Most of us have experienced an intense emotional state. As this emotion occurs, it seems to take over our existence—we feel we *are* the anger, love, hate. Only when we experience these intense states do we begin to dissipate the charge from the emotion. Then, we can step back, observe, and begin to notice we are separate from, and also the creator of, the intra-psychic experience. As Gertrude and Rubin Blanck illustrate in their research:

> "Here we see the relationship between mind as content as a result of boundaries in space. In fact, these boundaries are mind as content, and what constitutes psychic structure." (Blanck,1974:11).

The concept of self surrounded by boundaries is not a new one. However, within this self many part-(icles) or thoughtforms are contained, which is the way experiences are held solid like part-(icles). Since the observer created this structure, it is also able to dismantle it. The psychic structure of these part-(icles) is held in place in space. The self as we know it, or the aspects of the self in the content of the mind, begins to create a self-image, based on these held labels. As A.H. Almaas suggests:

> "Understanding the dynamic relation between self-image and space, we can theorize about the development of

psychic structures; the development of self-image simply represents a gradual building and constructing of boundaries in the mind space." (Almaas, 1986:34)

Since we all tend to identify ourselves with our experience, we begin to lose sight of the fact that we are more than the structures or images in our mind. The images often become the basis of our self-image. For example, a traumatic memory such as being slapped by an abusive parent becomes hypnotizing. It is labeled "bad," as we discussed before, and held in place. Different forms of therapy would take alternative methods to discharge this from the persons consciousness. Ericksonian therapy may center on re-framing the memory to orient the person to a different way of perceiving the experience. Gestalt therapy may work on the feelings left unfinished in the memory. Other forms may deal with the cognitive decisions made in the moment.

The Space

In order to look at this from a quantum perspective, it becomes necessary to include the space that surrounds the image or structure. This allows space for the picture to alter, and also allows the person more space to dis-identify from the memory. The observer can learn to include the space in his/her awareness. This space gives the observer more ability to observe the part-(icles) or thoughtforms arising in consciousness. This helps prevent the person from automatically fusing with the created structures and images, as we have illustrated before.

Quantum Exercise 26

• •

Step I: **Notice an old memory that keeps popping up in your consciousness, i.e., Mom/Dad doing X to you.**

Step II: **Observe the memory, noticing its shape.**

Step III: Allow your awareness to notice the space surrounding the memory (picture).

Step IV: Notice how the picture loses some of its charge when the space is included.

●●●●●●●●●●●●●●●●●●●●●●●●●●●●●●●

Because we see these memories and observe them, we forget we are the observer/creators as we fuse or become identified. The point is that we hypnotize ourselves into thinking we are these memories. To assist people to get back to zero, it is important to reach the ability to observe internal realities. This prevents the re-creation of feelings that you are *only* your memories. It allows the person to work with the part-(icles) or thoughtform and dismantle it, to experience the space that was initially present. Observation allows the thoughtforms to be perceived, the content of the thoughtform acknowledged and its size and shape to be seen. It allows the recognition that we are not the content of our minds.

Space is the substance that allows us to place experiences, such as part-(icle) realities, in a form. Without space there would be no way to contain experience. Imagine for a moment a photo album (See Chapter VII) that is one foot by two feet in size. Now, imagine a small snapshot that is pasted in the middle of the photo album. If the observer uses just the amount of awareness to see the photo, that is all that occupies his/her vision. If, however, the observer expands his/her awareness to include the entire one by two foot page, the picture loses its encompassing significance. Since the space around the photo is included, the picture or experience has a different context when it is viewed. The person becomes less identified with the picture. This is not to avoid the experience, but to understand that all our viewpoints are subjective in the way they are perceived or viewed. This can be practised when you go to a movie theatre. When you watch a movie, notice that the more you fuse with the story, the more real and exciting the movie feels. If I notice the black border of the wall or screen the movie is being projected on, the movie loses its charge. In short, when you include the space (in the movie theatre of your mind) the movie or image loses its significance. In essence, you see it as a movie rather than *real*.

Principle: All thoughts, feelings, emotions, associations, pictures, and experiences occur in space. (This will be discussed in detail in Chapter VII.)

Space becomes our commonality of experience but probably the least acknowledged, because our tendency is to merge with the picture, experience, and lose sight of the space that supports it. Space serves the important function of allowing us to place experiences, pictures, in our internal, cognitive reality. As demonstrated before in various quantum exercises, space is the constant factor; what emerges and disappears within the space is *transient* and can become a trance. As we begin to allow the spatial quality of our experiences, or part-(icles) floating in the ocean of space, we can begin to see that all part-(icles) or images come and go, and move within the context of space.

For example, by observing stars in the galaxy, you could imagine they can be part-(icles) floating in space. In our inner realities, we can watch our own stars or part-(icles) (thoughts) floating by—the thoughtforms that we occasionally grab and say, "This is me." This occurs as a particular thoughtform we allow ourselves to be identified with. If awareness is added by expanding the viewpoint to include space, then again we see the part-(icle), thoughtform, floating in space. We can then choose how to experience that reality or allow it to disappear into space.

Quantum Exercise 27

• •

Step I: Let your eyes close and sit quietly for a moment. Notice the space behind your eyes.

Step II: Next, as you observe, notice something may emerge in that space. It might be a thought, wish, fantasy, that grabs your attention, such as a relationship that is troubling you, a new job that is hoped for, what to eat for lunch, or a memory of a loved person.

Step III: Very gently notice the shape of these memo-
               ries (part-(icles)); notice the edge and form
               that goes with each one.

Step IV: Extend your consciousness out to include
               the space surrounding the shape.

Step V: Notice it can be viewed as a part-(icle) float-
               ing in space.

Step VI: Intentionally create the picture there sev-
               eral times. See how the observer impacts
               the experience.

• •

This picture can be created in the space repeatedly. This helps
the observer to "take charge" or take responsibility for holding,
putting, and keeping the memory (picture) there. This has to be done
without blame or shame. We are only asking the observer to
knowingly, consciously, intentionally create what he/she already
has created unconsciously. The picture appears to just happen to
come into his/her experience. But instead, the picture is placed
there. To move outside of an automatic reality, choice can be used
to create it intentionally. Now again notice the space around it,
which allows the creation. This allows more inner space.

In the above material we have been exploring the constructs in
our psyche that we have placed there and continue to manifest as a
solid and mass-like part-(icle). The space in consciousness that
allows for more choice can be attained or facilitated by the following exercise. This quantum exercise has evolved from many areas
and from many teachers. Many of these steps we have already
introduced and illuminated in the above material.

Quantum Exercise 28

• •

This exercise demonstrates an aspect of Einstein's *Special Theory of Relativity*: Energy is made of the same substance as mass. "When Einstein presented his special theory of relativity to the world in 1905, the entire concept of mass was transformed. With his famous equation $E=mc^2$, Einstein demonstrated that mass (m) is a form of energy (E); a particle such as an electron can be viewed as a lump of concentrated energy." (Davies,1992)

Step I: Observe there is something in your awareness that you don't want, i.e., a thought, feeling, emotion.

Step II: Notice the size, shape or dimension of the thought or feeling.

Step III: Notice its mass or solid nature like a particle.

Step IV: Intentionally merge with and become the part-(icle) within the shape.

Step V: Step-out of the shape and notice that you are the observer.

Step VI: Observe the shape as energy.

Step VII: Realize that the shape is a part-(icle) made of energy.

Step VIII: Observe what occurs when the part-(icle) is seen as energy.

• •

Below is a summary chart of where East, Middle East, and West intersect to form Quantum Psychology. The reader is encouraged to appreciate the roots of the tree of Quantum Psychology. The roots are old; the tree is a synthesis that allows all traditions to be appreciated for their contribution.

The zero point process and the appreciation that the observer is a participant in creating the reality he/she observes takes us to a greater sense of freedom. To move us even further along, however, we must realize that time becomes the next aspect to explore.

Quantum Psychology	Quantum Physics	Psychology	Oriental Healing and Esoteric Metaphysics	Buddhism	Yoga	Sufi	Western Philosophy
1. Feel and experience the emotion, thought, feeling or belief		Gestalt therapy Reichian therapy Bioenergetics Psychodrama		Tarthang Tulku *"Go directly into the emotion, become it, discover it, feel it thoroughly."*			
2. Notice the size, shape, and dimensions of the experience.	Bohm : *"all boundaries are observer created"*	Object relations: *all false selves have a boundary. Images are boundaried space.*	Edgar Cayce: *Thought Forms* Alice Bailey: *Thought Forms* C.W. Leadbeater and Anne Berant: *Thought Forms*			A.H. Almaas: *(1) Each self image has a shape and boundary. (2) You create and boundary yourself as a self.*	
3. Notice what is contained within the shape, (i.e., thoughts, feelings, memories, decisions, associations, etc.) and merge with it.		Transactional Analysis: *decisions-re-decisions* Freudian Psychoanalysis: *"All traumas occur in chains of earlier, similar events."*				G.I. Gurdjieff: *self-observation. Observe how the mind is organized.*	Constructionism: *You invent your reality.* Watzlawick: *The invented reality.* Ludwig Wittenstein
4. Notice the mass and solid nature of the part-(icle).	Bohm: *"The mass aspect of the universe."*	Reichian Therapy: *Body Armor* Bioenergetics: *Body Armor, Rolfing*					

	Physics	Psychology	Energy Healing	Buddhism	Advaita / Tantra	Fourth Way	Semantics
5. Merge with and be the part-(icle).		Gestalt Therapy: The Law of Paradoxical Change		Tarthang Tulku: "Go directly into the emotion, become it, discover it, feel it thoroughly."			Alfred Korzybski: (1) "The map is not the territory." (2) "Anything that you can know about cannot be you."
6. Step out of the shape and notice you are the observer.	Heisenberg: "Reality is observer created." J.A. Wheeler: The observer is actually a participator.	Psychosyntheses: "I have a mind, but I am not my mind." "I have feelings, but I am not my feelings." "I have a body, but I am not my body." "I am a pure center of self-consciousness and will."		Zen: Mindfulness Buddhism: Witnessing	Nisargadatta Maharaj: Witnessing Ramana Maharishi: Witnessing	G.I. Gurdjieff: Self observation	
7. De-label the part-(icle) and see it as energy.	Bohr: The universe is an unfolding and enfolding of energy, space, mass, and time. Einstein: Special Theory of Relativity: Energy is mass ($E=mc^2$)		C.W. Leadbeater: Chakras as spinning energy centers. Reiki Healing: Acupuncture: mass is energy condensed.		Tantric Yoga: Experiencing emotions as energy. Siva Sutras: World as a play of consciousness.		
8. Observe; what occurs as the part-(icle) is seen as energy.	Heisenberg: Reality is observer created. Bohr: "There is no quantum world, just a quantum description."		Tarthang Tulku: "If you watch it carefully, without involvement, you will see this emotion manifest in body and mind and then dissolve into pure energy."				Ludwig Wittgenstein: "Dismantling beliefs"

SIX

THE CONCEPT OF TIME

Time organizes our life, from getting up in the morning to when we eat and when we sleep. Time regulates our emotional stress levels such as feeling the "time crunch," or planning so that some time in the future we can retire or relax. More often than not, time determines our thinking and feeling states. Rumination about the past and what could have or should have been can cause depression; a looking back at the past time. Fantasies about future catastrophes or future dreams coming true can cause feelings of anxiety or elation. This illusive nature of Time, rarely questioned, and yet assumed as truth, organizes and determines how we live, think, and feel about ourselves.

As we take apart the fabric of quantum consciousness, it becomes important to look back at the threads in hindsight, so we can get a sense of where we were and where we are headed.

Level 1:   Developing the ability to be the observer of the wave-like nature of reality.

Level 2:   The world, both subjective and objective as made of energy.

Level 3:   You, as the observer and creator of experiences, label undifferentiated energy, to create part-(icles) or mass, which function as identities, false selves, emotional states, and beliefs.

Level 4

You are the observer/creator of the time aspect of consciousness.

Quantum Contemplation

Contemplate a universe where there is no concept of time.

Could a problem state exist if there were no time in which it could exist? Time, and the illusion of past, present, and future, traps us all in the web of limited existence. Volumes of books have been written about time, its nature. Even a Nobel Prize was awarded to Stephen Hawking and William Penrose for their "discovery" of the origin of time. Time also has become the subject of controversy in the holographic model of the brain, where past, present, and future happen not in a linear, left brain understanding of past, present, and future, but rather happen in the *now*, beyond time. For now, it will be sufficient to offer Quantum Psychology's very brief history of time, and more important, some exercises to experience oneself apart from the confines and limits of the concept and constraints of time. In Chapter VIII even deeper and more concise exercises will be conjoined to get you beyond time.

Quantum Psychology
and the Hologram

"A hologram is a three-dimensional photograph manufactured with the aid of a laser. To make a hologram, scientists first shine a laser bean on an object and then bounce a second laser beam off the reflected light of the first. Interestingly, it is the pattern of interference created by the two lasers that is recorded on a piece of film to create a hologram. To the naked eye, the image recorded on such a piece of film is a meaningless swirl. However, if another laser beam is shown through the developed film, the image reappears in all of its original and three-dimensional glory.

In addition to being three-dimensional, the image recorded in a hologram differs from a conventional photograph in another very important way. If you cut a normal photograph in half, each section will contain only half of the image that was contained in the original photograph. This is because each tiny section of the photograph, like each dot on a color television, contains only a single bit of information about the entire image. However, if you cut a hologram in half and then shine a laser though one of the sections, you will find that each half still contains the entire image of the original hologram. *Each tiny section of the hologram contains not only its own bit of information, but every other bit of information from the rest of the image as well.* Thus, you can cut a hologram up into pieces and each individual piece will still contain a blurrier but complete version of the entire picture. In other words, in a hologram, every part of the image inter-penetrates every other part in the same way that Bohm's non-local universe would interpenetrate all of its parts.

If Bohm is correct and the universe is a gigantic multi-dimensional hologram, such an underlying holographic order would have profound implications for many of our other common sense notions about reality. For example, in a holographic universe, time and space would no longer be viewed as fundamentals. Because the universe would be seen as possessing a deeper level in which concepts such as location break down, time and three-dimensional space ... would have to be viewed as projections of this deeper order. In other words, in the super-hologram of the universe, past, present, and future are all enfolded and exist simultaneously." (Talbot, 1987:46-47)

What does all this mean in simple English? If in fact the universe is a hologram, as Bohm suggests, and past, present, and future are all existing simultaneously, taken to the next logical extension, there is no time. Why is there no time? Because if everything is occurring simultaneously then there would only be NOW. Simply put, it would require an observer that would breakdown and decide there was a past, present, and future in order for there to be time (or beginning, middle, and an end).

Physicist David Bohm suggests,

"One is led to a new notion of unbroken wholeness which denies the classical analyzability of the world into separately and independently existing parts. The inseparable quantum interconnectedness of the whole universe is a fundamental reality." (Herbert, 1985:18)

This can best be understood by metaphor. Imagine that everything in the universe—you, your perceptions, feelings, the car, the moon, everything—is one large, *solid*, rubber ball. Billions of little pockets arise and subside on the surface of the ball. As a pocket arises it observes the world. Since the pockets observe the world, the world appears to be out there. The pockets naturally imagine they must be separate from the ball. Many times in each second these pockets go in and out of this rubber ball so that it appears as though there is just world out there, and little pockets (observers) over here. These little pockets (people) begin to explore this world, postulating how it got there, why it's there, and maybe their place in the world. The pockets (people) can never notice when they become the ball because there is no them to notice it or to be aware when it occurs. This is the universe; it only exists subjectively speaking, as long as you are there to be aware of it. This is the nature of time. Since there has to be the illusion of a *you* separate from the world, *deciding* that this unbroken wholeness is divided into a concept of past, a concept of present, and a concept of future.

Now, if there is no time, this has extraordinary implications. The first implication is that if there is no time, then there cannot be cause and effect, because cause and effect are linear and require a past, present, and future as a *time line*, linear construct. If everything is happening simultaneously, there could be no this in the past causing this in the present or future. Why? Because they would all just be occurring. (More about this in Chapter X).

For now, from a holographic point of view, it is impossible to say this or that in the past caused this or that effect in the present or future. This is a linear way of thinking. If we allow ourselves to just consider the possibility of no time and no cause and effect in the present or future, what would that mean? If there is no time, there is actually no order nor structured universe; there is just one undifferentiated consciousness. Gestalt Psychology research demonstrated that the brain organizes things in a linear way. This organization of things in a linear way presents the appearance of time as if there were a past, present, and a future. But if no time exists, there is no cause and effect and no past, present, and future.

"In terms of time, the universe as we perceive it, with its apparently separate succession of moments, would be the smear of ink once the turning handle has stretched it out into a long ribbon. We are not able to perceive that time, at the level of the super-hologram, possesses a coherent and unbroken structure, because that structure is enfolded or implicate in the level of the universe that we are privy to. Time and three-dimensional space are not the only processes Bohm feels are best explained as enfoldings and unfoldings in and out of the implicate order.

Perhaps the most intriguing aspect of Bohm's theory is how it might apply to our understanding of the human mind. As he sees it, if every particle of matter *interconnects* with every other particle, the brain itself must be viewed as

infinitely interconnected with the rest of the universe."
(Talbot, 1987:48-49).

This has important implications in the field of psychology,
since psychology has taken a reductionist position in regard to
problems. Most of us, who have been through some form of therapy
have looked at life through this reductionist position. By reductionist I mean that the therapist, presupposes that back then, in our past,
lies the problem, which is occurring right now (in the present). This
reduces cause and effect down to a simple Newtonian unit of past,
present, and future. Most forms of therapy *think, since thought
occurs and can only be linear,* that an event has a beginning, middle
and an end. Let's ask ourselves, "What if things aren't linear, cause
and effect and time bound? In *Quantum Reality,* by Nick Herbert,
we find:

> "*Quantum Reality #5:* Quantum logic (the world obeys a
> non-human kind of reasoning.)" (Herbert, 1985:20).

In the exercises that follow in this section and the rest of the
book, we are asked to consider the *What If,* and develop an
understanding beyond the mind.

> "Einstein threw out the classical concept of time. Bohr
> throws out the classical concept of truth. Our classical ideas
> of logic are simply wrong in a basic practical way. *The next
> step is to learn to think in the right way, to learn to think
> quantum-logically.*" (Herbert, 1985:21).

Noted scientist Pribram demonstrates that not only is everything connected to everything else, it is indicated that each "imagined"
individual brain has its own tuning systems through which it
translates light into a holographic image. This would mean that each
imagined self perceives its own individuality and experience through
the whole.

> "Pribram goes on to postulate that perhaps even at a level
> available to our perceptions, objective reality is holo-
> graphic and might be thought of as little more than a
> 'frequency domain.' That is, even the world we know may
> not be composed of objects. We may only be sensing

mechanisms moving through a vibrating dance of frequencies. Pribram suggests that the reason we translate this vibrating dance of frequencies into the solidity and objectivity of the universe as we know it is that our brains operate on the same holograhics-like principles as the dance of frequencies and is able to convert them into a picture much the same as a television converts the frequencies it receives into a more coherent image. As he puts it, 'I think the brain generates its own constructions and images of physical reality. But at the same time it generates them in such a way that they resonate with what really is there.'" (Osistynski, 70-73).

As an example, if we could imagine a super, three-dimensional movie of which we are all a part; the common factor is the light which passes through the projector and which is the implicate or underlying order. Each individual image on the screen translates that light within the light of the whole-(logram) into different frequencies, thus yielding different experiential realities. The brain of each individual sees only through the individual frequency, thus the *explicate order*. They do not see nor experience the implicate order (the light). The fascinating and wonderful fact is that the light, being the common factor, not only makes us all the same, but that in each "individual" brain, since it is a hologram, lies the entire universe or implicate order; in metaphysical terms, the macrocosm is in the microcosm and the microcosm is in the macrocosm. In Quantum Psychology terminology, the microcosm *is* the macrocosm, the macrocosm *is* the microcosm.

As Bohm sees it, this lack of distinct boundaries between what is alive and what is not once again underscores the inadequacy of a strictly mechanistic approach to the universe. Instead of trying to divide the universe into parts that are alive and parts that are not, a better approach might be to view the universe as an unbroken whole, a totality into which both living and nonliving things are constantly enfolding and unfolding.

What does all of this make of the mind-body problem? As Bohm sees it,

"If the universe is non-local at a sub-quantum level, that means that reality is ultimately a seamless web, and it is only our own idiosyncrasies that direct us to divide it up into such arbitrary categories as mind and body. Thus, consciousness cannot be considered as fundamentally separate from matter, any more than life can be considered as fundamentally separate from non-life. There is not dualism because both are secondary and derivative categories and both are enfolded in a higher common ground." (Talbot, 1987:53)

The impact on these discoveries should have an impact upon modern psychology.

Many schools of psychology look to handling the past as a way to solve the present problem. This is implied through most schools of therapy. I should add that the purpose of this discussion is not to criticize psychology or spiritual practice. Rather, the purpose is for all of us to join hands in the development of a form of "inner work" that includes the world of Quantum Physics.

In Ericksonian hypnosis, a favorite technique is asking a client's unconscious to see a future where the problem is already resolved. Then the client is given suggestions to notice *how* they handled the problem, taking back to the present resources from the imagined future.

In this type of work, the future is treated as now and can be experienced that way in trance or my no-trance state. To illustrate this, recently, I had a discussion over the phone with noted Ericksonian therapist Stephen R. Lankton. Lankton not only acknowledged Erickson's utilization of time but also said, "by putting the imagined future in the present-time experience, we are putting the 'how to change' of the future in the present." This means, that we are putting the "alleged future in the present." This approach often helps in problem resolution as we look past the limits of what we normally construe as linear time. Dr. Milton H. Erickson, had many approaches in shifting time around, that helped alleviate problems that were being presented in his clinical practice. The difference between Quantum Psychology and Erickson's work, (although Erickson's work somehow acknowledges that the time is more transparent, more fluid, more expandable than most forms of therapy), is that Erickson is still dealing with shifting problems and creating identities. There is nothing wrong with creating identities or changing problems or solving problems. The thing is, if you have a problem called "intimacy", i.e., you cannot get too close to people without feeling afraid, in the Erickson model, you would want to develop some kind of resources or re-association. This would help make it okay to be intimate. This means you are saying it is better to be intimate than not intimate. That is a *judgment*. Quantum Psychology merely notes that these are two particular things in conflict, i.e. identity part-(icle) called "no intimacy" and identity part-(icle) called "intimacy". Here, once again, I am using the word part-(icle) because any experience can only occur if a part is viewed as separate from the whole. Ultimately, these identities are part-(icles) floating in empty space, and these part-(icles) are *not* floating in empty space, because the space and the part-(icles) are the same substance. (This will be discussed in later chapters.)

Erickson's work acknowledges the fact that the future is taking place right now just as the past is taking place right now. Erickson attempts to somehow change the present, or use the future, into something more acceptable now. What we are suggesting is moving people beyond their identification with any particular problem states, or part-(icle), so they can take responsibility for their own, subjective creations, and stop creating them. This allows individuals to see the whole. Most psychology, however, separates past, present, and future, and has not evolved a psychology on the holographic model. This book attempts to bring a transformation to psychology, so that the whole or quantum unity is acknowledged and is viewed as a context for the parts. (More about this in Chapters IX and X.)

How do we take the beginning steps to go beyond time? Let us refer back to the last chapter, *Getting to Zero*.

Step I: *Practice* zero point and notice yourself as the creator/observer. Watch the size and shape of the part-(icle), belief or experience.

Step II: As you notice that emotion, thought, memory, etc. inside the part-(icle), notice that the observer that's watching is there and is actually not in time, but that the part-(icle) appears to exist in time. You, however, are outside time. Thoughts, emotions, memories, or part-(icles) are in time.

Quantum Contemplation

Contemplate that since you can observe time, you are separate from and exist not in time. For example, notice that you feel that you have never changed. Or consider, that as you look in the mirror the person *seems* older, but you seem unchanged.

Quantum Exercise 29

• •

Look into a mirror and be the observer. Notice that the person has changed in time. Notice that if you don't use your memory, you experience yourself as unchanged.

• •

Why is this phenomenon so widely reported? Because at some level we feel ourselves as observers and as outside of, and unaffected by, time. Furthermore, memory is in the context of time. If we don't use our memory we experience ourselves out of time or in a no-time space. This also explains why we have such a denial of death. Since we, the observer, do not experience ourselves in time, we do not fear time coming to an end.

Quantum Contemplation

Without using memory, thoughts, or associations are you in time, out of time, or neither?

How to Remove Yourself from Time-Bound Beliefs

Since time is a concept and is organized by you, the word time in and of itself brings up countless beliefs. For example, "I never have enough time," "there isn't enough time," "I am running out of time," or "time is money." For some reason, we all, when you use the word time make time a frozen experience, "as if" time was not a concept, and time was a fact and stationary, or a noun rather than a *verb*. To loosen the parameters of time the following exercise has been adapted.

Quantum Exercise 30

● ●

The concept of time.

Since time is a concept, change the word "time" to the word "existence."

The rotating group facilitator may use this format:

As you begin to use this method, first look at the concepts of time that you have. Look at the concept of time and all your beliefs about time. You can start with, "Time is _____" and fill in the blanks. Keep repeating "Time is_____" until you have a list of beliefs. Notice all of your concepts about time. Go back over your concepts of time, but change the word "time" to the word "existence." For instance, you might believe, "There isn't enough time for me." See what it does for your experience when you change the word "time" to the word "existence." For example, rather than "there isn't enough time for me" you change it to, "there isn't enough existence for me.

● ●

Here are some comments I've received from students in my workshops.

"Well, I got a feeling that time is something that we invented to ground us."

"I got, 'time is short, and when you said change it to 'existence,' existence is timeless, and I stayed on that for a long time."

"I started flashing on Japan and the bullet train, and it's always right on time. It's very important to the Japanese, but this bullet train is always accurate, always on time. And I started thinking about all of the watches that come out of Japan."

"I found that the concept of time started out in an intellectual place, and then I found that time is limiting, and I started feeling very angry at the whole concept of time. And when I switched it to existence, the anger went away."

As we have already discussed, everything that appears, appears to have a duration or beginning, a middle, and an end. For example, if you feel sad, you can notice that the sadness had a beginning (when it started), a middle (when it was most intense), and an end (when it began to dissipate and go away). This can be likened to what a Yogi might call, "creation, sustaining, and destroying." In the Yoga tradition there are thousands of gods and goddesses, each responsible for some aspect of consciousness: the creator (of an experience) is called Brahma; the sustaining force, Vishnu, and the destroyer, Shiva. What Hindus noticed along with quantum physicists was that time was essential. Stated in Quantum Psychological terminology:

Principle: Everything that appears in the physical universe has the appearance of time (duration), a beginning, a middle, and an end.

This is why Bohm sees time as a major aspect of consciousness. If there were no time, there would be no time in which something could exist.

Quantum Contemplation

Contemplate that if there were no time, then there would be no time in which a problem could exist.

How could this be applied to practical experience? If we are experiencing a feeling and begin to observe it's appearance of duration, the feeling will dissipate and disappear. This is because in order for you to notice and witness the time-bound aspect of experience, you would have to step out of the time aspect that is intrinsic to any experience. Basically, in order to observe time, you have to step outside and observe it. This allows an unwanted thought, i.e., "What's wrong with me?" to run its course. By doing this you are getting out of the way of the thought and allowing it to occur without resisting it or trying to change it. This allows the experience to have movement and be a verb, rather than a frozen noun. *The observer is outside of time, since he/she can observe time.* The following exercise will help to make this more experiential.

Quantum Exercise 31

● ●

Noting the impact of time on created reality.

Step I: Notice a thought that goes by.

Step II: As you notice the thought label the beginning of the thought "Beginning."

Step III: Label the intense part of the experience "Middle."

Step IV: Label its ending "Ending."

● ●

To do this exercise, a person need only notice any experience they are having and then label, according to the experience, its beginning, its middle, or its ending. What this serves to do is that in order to notice the time aspect of an experience, you have to step out of time, and get in the observation mode. This takes you out of the time constraints, out of being stuck. You can become separate from time, i.e., observing, and secondly, once you notice where the experience is, (beginning, middle and end), it takes *you* out of being in it and out of the time aspect. For example, when you are in an experience like anxiety, it feels like "it will never end." By noticing, however, its place in the time continuum you are put outside of the effect of time. This frees you and frees the experience to not appear *time* frozen. When you fuse with an experience, you feel time. Why? Because all experiences occur in time. Therefore, when you move from being the observer of an experience (the observer of a time-bound experience is not in time) to being an experience, you feel like you are in time and frozen. Observing experiences moves you into a no-time space, and allows for the *movement* of an experience.

Quantum Exercise 32

• •

Step I: Notice or recall an emotion.

Step II: As you notice the emotion label the beginning of the emotion "Beginning."

Step III: Label the intense part of the emotional experience "Middle."

Step IV: Label its ending "Ending."

• •

Quantum Exercise 33

• •

Step I: Notice a feeling that goes by and see the thought or feeling as energy.

Step II: As you notice the feeling, label the beginning of the thought "Beginning" while seeing the thought or feeling as energy.

Step III: Label the intense part of the experience "Middle" while seeing the thought or feeling as energy.

Step IV: Label its ending "Ending" while seeing the thought or feeling as energy.

• •

How Crucial is Time?

In the psychotherapy of Milton H. Erickson, Erickson noticed that the experience of pain was so awful *because* of this "time" continuum. Dr. Erickson, being a master of pain control, noticed in his clinical practice that the experience of physical pain has three parts: past remembered pain, present pain, and fear of the pain extending into the future. Erickson noted that if he got the patient to let go of past remembered pain, and the fear of recurring future pain, he could diminish the physical discomfort by two-thirds. In the same way, in the time continuum, labeling any experience "beginning", "middle", and "end", takes you out of the time continuum so you can observe time and its fluid motion. This allows the experience to run its time-bound course. By not resisting and just allowing its natural flow from beginning in time to disappearing out of time, frees you from the identification with constraints and limitations of time-bound reality. The greater subtlety of time and its illusive effects will be demonstrated in Chapter IX.

Conclusion

The purpose of this chapter is to loosen the concept of time. As mentioned earlier, Bohm suggests that the world is an unfolding and enfolding of energy, space, mass, and time. For our purposes, nothing can exist within the physical universe if one of these components is not there. Therefore, removing yourself from a time, energy or mass experience, moves you away from any time-locked, frozen limitations.

As with all of this work, keeping open to possibility, permits us to reconsider our constructed limitations.

SEVEN

SPACE: THE FINAL FRONTIER

Many of us can recall the beginning of *Star Trek* and certainly the words of Captain Kirk, "Space: the Final Frontier." This section will explore and introduce "Inner Space: the Final Frontier."

In the last several chapters, we have experienced both the inner and outer possibilities and meanings of energy, mass, time and wave/particle aspects of the universe. We examined the world of inner experience as composed of energy, mass, and time. This section offers an introduction into one of the most interesting and least talked about areas of consciousness, space. Why is space so relevant and yet overlooked?

Level 5

Going beyond the space aspect of consciousness.

Let's look at this in terms of Quantum Psychology principles.

***Principle*:** In order for anything (thoughts, feelings, chairs, cars, etc.) to exist in the physical universe, there must be a space to put it in.

At first this seems rather abstract, but upon closer investigation, we can notice, for example, that our body has a space that it occupies. If there were no space in which to put a body, the body would have no place to exist, or *be* in.

Quantum Contemplations

(eyes closed)

Contemplate just for a moment a universe in which there were no space to put anything in.

Contemplate where, if anywhere, an "internal" problem state (anger or upset, etc.) could exist if there were no space for it to exist in.

Contemplate where, if anywhere, an "external" object (chair, floor, house, body, etc.) could exist if there were no space for it to exist in.

Surprised? Nothing can exist in the physical universe without a space to put it in!!

What is space? If you close your eyes for just a moment, you can see an empty space in front of you. Now, you can watch and see a thought go by such as, "Yeah, so what if it's true, who cares?" except that this thought could only exist if there were a place or space for it to exist *in*. No space, no thought. Albert Einstein, in his Special Theory of Relativity, demonstrated that space and matter were the same. What will be experientially offered here are introductory exercises, so that this experience of space can become readily available along with how to apply it and transform our subjective experience of reality. As a note, it would be impossible to offer all the processes of the Quantum Psychology® four-day workshop on energy, space, mass, and time, in the limits of this book. It is hoped that these exercises will emphasize the importance of space as a major aspect of consciousness and hence the world, both inner and outer, along with the implications and applications as we include and acknowledge space.

Quantum Aerobics

Quantum Exercise 34

● ●

(Open eyed)

Step I: Look at an object in the room, then withdraw your attention from it, prior to the thought or impression of the object. (Singh, 1979:107)

● ●

The next two exercises are open-eyed. The first one involves practice with objects in the room. When you try this, you might want to practice in a small group. This enables us to make eye contact with a partner and then switch to another partner. This permits contact to be made *space* to *space* rather than person to person. Opening up this space-to-space connection deepens contact and intimacy, because it removes created personal internal obstacles.

• •

Practice

Format rotating group facilitator may use:

Pick an object in the room, like a chair. Begin to pull your attention backward, into the space *prior* to your knowledge of the object. In other words, your attention is normally experienced as going forward or outward toward a particular object, like the couch or person. Pull your attention back inside, or backward toward the back of your head. As you look at an object, pull your attention back to the space in back of your head, prior to the impression, idea, or thought of the object.

• •

A workshop participant once commented, "I can go backward prior to the impression of the object but I still see its color." I replied, "You will continue to see the color, but it will no longer register as, say, the rug in the living room. In other words, the color is still there and it's not going to disappear, but you're moving, withdrawing your attention past the thought and impression, even the knowledge of it. IT IS A VERY DEEP FOCUS, to the space prior to the knowing."

One student said, "I feel like I go back to the back of my head and have to stay there in order to get it. "Exactly," I replied, "you pull your attention to the space, *prior to* the knowledge of the object arising."

The point of this exercise is to get you to the space prior to thoughts or impressions or even knowledge of an object. This allows us to appreciate the space that is constant and yet goes unnoticed and unacknowledged. These quantum aerobics allow us to experience the space that is always there, the space we all share.

Once we can appreciate the space that we all live in, we can begin to enjoy the *medium* or the substance that connects us all. For example, let's say, we are in a swimming pool and that it appears, at an explicate level, that I am separate from you. We experience fear, anger, loneliness, etc. If however, we get in touch with the water as our common connection, we can appreciate not only how we are connected, but that we live in the same, interconnected space (the water) and hence, effect each other. To illustrate, if I am in a swimming pool relaxing on my air mattress, and somebody does a cannonball dive, I am made wet, bumped around, and maybe even knocked off into the water. If I can begin to acknowledge the shared common unity (the water), we might change our actions environmentally as well as emotionally. Why? Because everything shares a common space. What makes this quite different from most psychological and spiritual practices is that in psychology you are concerned with the "content" of what occurred. This is often called the "foreground". In spiritual disciplines, the focus is on moving beyond the foreground (thoughts, desires, etc.). Many people are considered less than pure, not ready, unevolved because their foreground is looked upon as "bad" or something that needs to be changed. Quantum Psychology asks the practitioner to focus on the changeless *background* (implicate order). Why? Because the foreground (explicate order) always changes, while the background, or implicate order, remains the same. But, getting in touch with the background, and acquiring a taste for it, changes the context of your life—interconnection is enhanced and pain of separation decreases.

Quantum Exercise 35

• •

Practice

Group facilitator: ("pair up with a partner for this next exercise.")

In my workshops, I often jokingly say, "Pair up with someone you are unconsciously repulsed by," or "Pair up with someone you are unconsciously attracted to." Keep the exercises light. This is supposed to be fun.

Let your eyes close for a second, then make eye contact with your partner. Let your attention withdraw, pulling your awareness backward to the space prior to knowledge, information, impressions, or thoughts you

have about that person. Turn your attention inside, withdrawing it backward, toward the back of your head. Notice the space prior to your impression of the other person. Let your eyes close again. Make eye contact with another person, and again gently withdraw your attention, prior to any thoughts or impressions or information you have about that person. Find the space before any thoughts or information.

• •

A workshop participant commented, "It was like I was feeling the back of my head from the inside. I was looking from back there (points to back of head)."

A student said, "Everything went out of focus and my partner's eyes looked purple. It was really interesting because what I noticed was that there was this great big light around everything as soon as that moment of complete detachment comes."

Another participant commented, "The focusing happened very fast for me. Suddenly I was pulsating back and forth, and I was focusing very fast."

There are two things to be said in response to this feedback. Pulsating is "spanda," which as mentioned in Chapter IV, is a Sanskrit term meaning "the divine pulsation" or "the divine throb." Second, while in deep focusing, everything loses its form because we make a form like anger or sadness more solid by our label. When you pull your attention back subjectively, it loses its solidness, its label, because you are seeing it from the space, rather than from your ideas or impressions about the object or person.

This is a good practice to use if you're in a relationship with somebody and you're in the middle of an argument. If you can remember to do this exercise with them, begin by looking at them and pulling your attention *backward* prior to any impressions or even knowledge about that person. To do this you have to be willing to drop all your concepts about how right you are and move past any impressions, information or knowledge you have about that other person—to see them from the space *prior to*. This practice will begin to dissolve the problem because you move into the space from which the problem has arisen, or prior to the existence of the problems. You can practice this all of the time. Seeing and experiencing the space prior to the problem helps us to re-member, or become a member again in the common space of which we are all members.

Quantum Exercise 36

• •

Step I: Notice a thought or feeling you are having.

Step II: Withdraw your attention from the thought or feeling prior to any knowledge or information about what the thought or feeling is.

Step III: View the thought or E-motion from that space as if you are seeing the thought or feeling for the first time.

• •

In the classic, *Zen Mind, Beginner's Mind*, by Shunryu Suzuki, he is asking for a beginner's mind to see things anew for the first time.

"The mind of the beginner is needed throughout Zen practice. It is an open mind, the attitude that includes both doubt and possibility, the ability to see things always as fresh and new. It is needed in all aspects of Life. Beginner's mind is the Practice of Zen Mind."

This is what we are asking, to pull your attention back past all knowledge of internal thoughts, feelings, or external chairs, or windows and see something from the space *prior to* the knowledge of the occurrence. This is beginner's mind.

Quantum Exercise 37

• •

Walk around looking at objects, people, thoughts, E-motions "as if" this were the first time you had ever seen them.

• •

As I mentioned earlier, I was once in India with a teacher, Nisargadatta Maharaj. He asked a woman, who was making an audio tape of his talk for a new book, "What is the name of my next book?" She replied, "Beyond Consciousness." He said, "No, *Prior to Consciousness*. Find the space prior to your thought and stay there."

This exercise illustrates the same idea. Prior to any impression, there is space, the generally overlooked implicate order, which connects us all. Often people complain, "I need my space." Space is yours. Nobody can take it away. It is more of a shift in focus to notice that space is where you come from. You already have your own space. You just need to acknowledge it.

Everything in the world has a space, and what you can do is withdraw your attention from people, situations, and objects, so that you have your space back.

A workshop participant asked, "Isn't this withdrawing from the person and the world, like dissociating?" I said, "No, dissociation is an automatic defense, usually created during a trauma, to defend against someone or something. In this practice, we are *connecting* space to space. We are acknowledging the space we all share. This creates an entirely new context for relationship, since, your point of departure is the interconnected wholeness of the space (implicate order), rather than the separation and fear of the explicate order. In this approach, we are acknowledging our connection and similarities first, and separation and differences second, rather than our habit of doing it the other way around."

Quantum Exercise 38

• •

Step I: Move your eyes quickly from object to object and find the space between two objects.

Practice

All objects and experiences have a space. Also, as mentioned in Chapter III, there is a space between two objects. By locating the space between two objects, whether they are thoughts, feelings, chairs, or tables, we

get back in touch with our common underlying space. This can offer us a feeling of interconnection and an experience of harmony.

Let your eyes move rapidly, eyes open, from object to object in the room very quickly. Find the space between two objects. As you focus on one object and then another, there is a space. Find the space between two objects by allowing your eyes to move very rapidly.

Once again notice how the space is overlooked.

• •

One workshop participant commented, "It was like looking at frames in a movie or a slide show; as I moved my eyes from object to object, the space between the frames jumped out at me." I replied, "The space on which the slide show appears is overlooked; that is the implicate order or background."

What always gets emphasized is the slide show or story in our life. Obviously, it is impossible to feel "secure," if we focused on the slide show (the foreground). It is only possible if we focus on the changeless background.

Quantum Exercise 39

• •

Acknowledging the space around mental images.

Format rotating group facilitator may consider:

Practice

Let your eyes close and notice the empty space. Now create an image of the beach. Allow the beach to become real with feelings, sounds of waves, maybe even a temperature change, and experience it.

Now notice how in order to experience this image, you have to not notice the background or space. Expand your awareness and notice the space that surrounds the experience. Observe how the experience loses its potency when the background or space is included. Why? Because you are expanding your awareness to include the changeless space. In psychological terms, you are de-potentiating the picture or story by including the space in which it occurs or the background.

● ●

As another illustration: (mentioned in Chapter V) imagine looking at a photograph album with different pictures in it. If you exclude the background or page on which the pictures are mounted, the pictures seem more intense. If you shift your awareness, like a zoom lens camera, and include the page that the picture is on, the picture looses its intensity. This is the de-potentiating of a story, picture, or memory that you hold in your consciousness. In Ericksonian terms it would be called the de-potentiating of conscious mind sets.

What this means in the context of Quantum Psychology® is that in our life, we take pictures of the traumas in our life (rape, incest, etc.), and literally hold them in front of our face and relate to the world through them. For example, a man who was molested by his mother might hold that memory of being taken advantage of, and relate to women with that expectation. Around women he might get scared, frozen, or withdraw. This is the mind-set which causes post traumatic stress disorder (P.T.S.D.). By expanding and including the space in which the picture exists as the context which holds the picture, the frozen stuckness of the memory is reduced. This allows the person to relate to women through a larger window than just that one picture-window. This reduces his P.T.S.D. and de-potentiates his mind set, thus expanding his world view.

How to apply this with yourself, or, if you are a therapist, with another ,will be demonstrated in Chapter IX.

Quantum Exercise 40

• •

From space to form.

Step I: Letting your eyes close, see the space.

Step II: Open your eyes and see the physical objects.

Step III: While looking at the outer forms, keep part
             of your attention on the space. Let your eyes
             close for a second, and see the space. And
             when your eyes are open, see the outer
             world.

Practice

Group facilitator:

For a second, let your eyes open and see the outer world.
Now, let your eyes close and see the inner world. Let
your eyes be open, and world will appear. Let your eyes
close, and see the space. Continue to open and close your
eyes until you can keep the background of the space as
you look at people and objects.

• •

Once you can "get" the space (inner) and world (outer), let your
attention be split. This means have your attention on the world
outside *and* on the space inside simultaneously. This takes practice,
but as you begin to develop this skill, you can stay in touch with the
outer world and the inner world simultaneously. Often, most of us
in relationships loose our space by focusing on our partner. Others
of us, lose our connection with our relationship because we stay in
the space. Thus the double bind of either, "I have a relationship and
lose myself," or "I have myself and I am alone, and don't have a
relationship." This creates conflicts that arise in relationships

constantly. Often I am asked in workshops, "How can I have myself (my own space) and have a connection with another (relationship)?"

This exercise suggests you can have both by splitting your attention inside and outside, so they are equally balanced. P. D. Ouspensky, a noted mystic and well-known student of Sufi teacher G. I. Gurdjieff, suggests this approach.

> "When I pay attention to the external world, I am like an arrow pointing outwards. When I close my eyes and sink into myself my attention becomes an arrow pointing inwards. Now, I try to do both at once—to point the arrow in and out at the same time—I immediately discover that this is incredibly difficult. After a second or two, I either forget the outside world, and sink into a daydream, or forget myself and become absorbed in what I am looking at." (Wilson,1980)

This approach, asks the practitioner to do precisely this technique of self-remembering. To focus on the space (inside) and the outer world (outside) simultaneously, and balanced.

This is a nice exercise, particularly in relationships, to help stay in touch with your space and your partner simultaneously, or just at the same time.

Quantum Exercise 41

● ●

The space at the end of a sound.

Step I: **Focus your attention on the space at the end of a word, a sentence, a voice, or any sound.**

● ●

We are looking for the space that is usually unnoticed. Most of us focus on the words and what they mean to us. This is focus on the foreground (more on this in Chapters IX and X), rather than focusing on the background or the space that is always there and is the same for us all.

We are working with being able to utilize voice, words, sentences that we hear, in essence, using everything that occurs in our inner and outer world. These exercises can be very valuable in beginning to put us in touch with this changeless, unified space. One of the distinguishing characteristics between this and other disciplines is that other disciplines require that you schedule in a time to do a particular "practice." In Quantum Psychology, you can live your life and enter into the space just by *shifting where you put your attention*. In this exercise whether you hear a voice, a plane going overhead, traffic sounds, a voice inside your head, or the space at the end of this word, find the space at the end of the sound and stay there. If you're listening to a sentence in your mind or to an idea, find the space at the end of the sound. You're going to sort of drop into that space, that silence, that void.

● ●

Practice

The person who is acting as the group facilitator reads the exercise out loud, very slowly. This allows the participants to focus on the space between his words.

Let yourself drop into the space or the void after the utterance of my voice, the word, or an idea, or any sound, or notice the space at the end of a written word. Stay in that space. Use every sound inside or outside yourself and find the space at the end of it. Anytime you want to practice this exercise all you have to do, whether you're driving your car, shopping, or just going about your daily errands, is stay focused on the space at the end of each word or sound, even in a conversation. This will connect you to the underlying space or background that is always present *right now*.

● ●

For homework, I often suggest that we spend some time, in the next week or so, finding the space at the end of conversations, rather than focusing on the words. In other words, in conversation, focus on the background or space at the end of someone's words rather than the words themselves.

As we mentioned in Chapter II, all of us are mostly composed, at a subatomic level, of space and particles. This next exercise gets us in touch with the body as space. By doing this exercise, even at a physical level we can open up the possibility that we are all surrounded by and made up of the same interconnected space.

Quantum Exercise 42

●●●●●●●●●●●●●●●●●●●●●●●●●●●●●●

Focus on your skin as being solid. Notice it's mass-like quality.

Consider there is nothing but space inside it.

Format for a group facilitator:

Let your eyes close. Focus your attention on your skin boundary, your physical skin boundary. I'd like you to experience and focus your attention on your skin as though it were solid, as though it were a solid mass. As you focus your attention on your skin as though it were solid, notice its texture, what it's made out of. Notice how it feels and looks.

Next, contemplate that there is nothing but space inside it. As you feel the solidness and see how it looks, contemplate that there's nothing but space inside it. Very gently, bring your awareness back to the room.

●●●●●●●●●●●●●●●●●●●●●●●●●●●●●●

One workshop participant said, "Just seeing inside as empty space really quieted my mind down." I replied, "All the exercises are attempts to open up a new eye of perception and a new possibility."

In Chapter IV, we had exercises in which the skin boundary is experienced as energy. In this chapter, let's explore the space aspect of the skin boundary.

"There are two views of space. One view is to say the skin boundary of ourselves, saying there's the space without and the space within. The space within is the separate self, obviously, and the space without the space that separates the separate selves. To overcome that separation, you must have a process of moving through that space. (David Bohm, *The Enfolding-Unfolding Universe: a Conversation with David Bohm*).

Using David Bohm's suggestion, lets look at two more quantum exercises as ways to overcome separation.

Quantum Exercise 43

• •

Step I: Let your eyes close, and feel your skin boundary like a wall. (Singh, 1979:43-44)

Step II: Contemplate the space within the wall.

Step III: Contemplate and experience the wall as made of the same space as the space inside.

After a few moments, gently, bring your awareness back to the room.

• •

Quantum Exercise 44

• •

The universe as space.

Step I: Let your eyes close again and experience your skin boundary as solid and mass-like.

Step II: Experience the space inside this mass-like structure called the skin-boundary.

Step III: Next, experience the space outside the mass-like skin-boundary.

Step IV: Now, experience the space inside the mass-like skin-boundary, the skin-boundary, and the space outside the skin-boundary as all being the same space.

● ●

Quantum Exercise 45

● ●

The space of the body.

Step I: Imagine your physical body as empty space. (Singh, 1979:43)

Practice (eyes closed)

Group facilitator:

Focus your attention on your physical body as though it were empty space. Imagine your skin, your flesh, your body, and bones as empty space. With your eyes closed, enjoy the experience of your body as empty space.

After several minutes, gently feel your body, feel where it is, notice your breathing, and very gently, bring your awareness back to the room. When you're ready, let your eyes open.

● ●

A student commented, "I was experiencing that everything is a manifestation of something else, and that I am space. It was as if the space was there, and I didn't have to do anything. It was a relief."

Quantum Exercise 46

• •

Step I: **Get in touch with the space "inside."**

Step II: **Look at objects in the room, and imagine them as particles floating in empty space.**

• •

This exercise offers us the opportunity to slip on the "quantum lens," and view the spacious world and what we call objects as particles, with no boundaries no definitions, floating in empty space. This exercise can be done eyes open, not blinking, and by pulling your attention backward as in Quantum Exercise 34. It is important to notice that if we look at the world from "back there," prior to thoughts, impressions, or knowledge of an object or ourself—the space becomes more available and boundaries disappear. Why? Because we are looking without using our memory or mind—we are just looking. The memories, which are accumulated pictures of the world and ourself puts boundaries and "freezes" the subjective experience of ourself and the world. Looking without the mind, moves us outside the concepts of energy, space, mass and time—hence no boundaries!

One student said, "At first it was difficult, but as I allowed myself to open up to the possibility, I was able to do it."

Another workshop participant said, "It was difficult for me, too, but as I allowed it, I could see the space, even with eyes open. What was awesome was that there were times where the space was so pervasive I couldn't tell if my eyes were open or closed."

Here, I am including comments that support the exercise. It is a difficult practice, but one need only to consider, permit, be willing, or allow this "quantum lens" to slip on as a possibility.

Quantum Exercise 47

• •

The space in all directions. (Singh, 1979:41)

This exercise is done in a group, with one group member leading, as a guide.

Possible format for a group facilitator.

(Eyes closed)

Feel your body being supported, and notice your breath rising and falling. With eyes closed, focus on the space above you as though outer space were directly above you. Focus your attention on the space above you. Keep your attention on the space above you. Now, focus your attention on the space below you. Focus your attention on the void below you. Continue to focus your attention on the void below you. Now, focus your attention on the space just to the right of you. Focus your attention on the void just to your right. Now, I'd like you to focus your attention on the space on the left. Now, focus your attention on the space in front of you, almost as though you're looking into the space; and focus all of your attention on the void in front of you, completely in front of you, almost as if you're sitting on the edge, looking into space.

In one gesture, let the space be simultaneously in front of you, behind you, above you, below you, and in all directions, inside of you and outside of you, in all directions. Let everything be space all at once, simulta-neously in all directions, everything as a void. Continue to focus your attention on the space extending in every direction, all at once, simultaneously.

• •

Quantum Exercise 48

• •

Merging space.

(Eyes closed.)

Step I: Notice the space below you.

Step II: Notice the space to your left.

Step III: Notice the space to your right.

Step IV: Notice the space above you.

Step V: Notice the space outside your body.

Step VI: Notice the space inside your body.

Step VII: See the inner and outer space as the same
              space.

Group facilitator:

Take this space that is surrounding your body and
notice the empty space inside your body. Notice how the
empty space inside the body is the same as the empty
space outside the body. Now, allow the inner space and
outer space to merge, so that all that is left is space.

With you as the observer or witness of space, realize
that you determine what you call *inside of yourself* and
what you call *outside yourself* by decision. Also, notice
what you call *you* and what you call *not you* is a
subjective decision. Notice, that since you are the observer of space, you are not in space, but outside of
space.

Notice your breath, letting it come up to your chest just a little bit, and then feel your body being physically supported by the couch, the seat, by the floor. And very gently, whenever you're ready, let your eyes begin to open.

● ●

One student commented, "I felt like I and everything else was just space."

Another participant said, "It was difficult at first, and my mind did not want to get it, but, as I went along with your words, I felt like all there was, was space."

What is the importance, of seeing particles and energy moving through space?

"Our objective reality is composed of a void full of pulsating fields. If we stop the pulsation of the fields, we get back to the absolute. (Bentov, 1977:67).

Conclusion

These exercises, which can be done in a group, in pairs, or on your own, can open the possibility of becoming aware of a world of interconnected space. This space, once acknowledged, can become a constant recognition of the space in which we all live, a major quantum jump, our next quantum jump in the relationship between the space and the apparent energy or particles we call ourselves.

EIGHT

THE LIVING
VOID

Turn off your mind relax and float down stream ... it is not dying, it is not dying...Lay down all thought surrender to the void ... it is shining, it is shining.

John Lennon

As we begin to move further along in our journey, we can appreciate that in order for anything to exist in the physical universe, it must have energy, occupy a space, have solidness, and have a time (duration). What the last exercises were intended to do was to give us an experience of being beyond the concepts of energy, space, mass, and time. This provides us with a new pair of glasses, our "quantum lens," so that we can pierce the apparent nature of the physical universe, and discover our true nature.

The question still arises then, "Who Am I?" But, as we bring the answer to that question more and more into focus, we can notice that we are the ones who are witnessing the energy, space, mass, and time, and as mentioned in Chapter I, anything that you can observe, you are separate from. To repeat the words of Alfred Korzybski, "Anything you know about can't be you," or, "The map is not the territory."

Level 6

You are beyond the aspects of
energy, space, mass, and time.

Being the observer and the participator in the creation of energy, space, mass, and time, brings us to another hilltop from which to view reality. As Einstein demonstrated,

"Everything is made of emptiness and form is condensed emptiness."

What does this mean? Well, before we go on to explore experientially what it means, let us say that energy is the same as matter, and that space is the same as matter, energy and time. Einstein proved, that everything is made of the same substance; i.e., emptiness being form, form being emptiness. As mentioned in Chapter I, the *Buddhist Heart Sutra* says it exactly the same way: "Form is none other than emptiness, emptiness is none other than form."

In *Quantum Field Theory*, the distinction between particles and space surrounding them loses its original sharpness, and the void is recognized as a dynamic quantity of paramount importance. In Einstein's field equations, matter cannot be separated from its field of gravity, and the field of gravity cannot be separated from the curved space. Matter and space are thus seen to be inseparable and interdependent parts of a single whole. Modern physics shows us once again that material objects are not distinct entities but are inseverable links to the environment, that their properties can only be understood in terms of the interaction with the rest of the world. A quantum field is a field which can take the form of quanta or particles.

Quantum field is seen as the fundamental physical entity, a continuous medium which is present everywhere in space." (Capek, 1961:319).

Before we go into its far reaching effects, and offer exercises, I wanted to clarify that I will be using the terms "quantum field", "void", and "emptiness" as synonyms.

Quantum Exercise 49

● ●

Einstein's riddle.

Step I: Notice a conflict you are having, i.e., to stay in a relationship, not to stay in a relationship.

Step II: Notice the shape and size of each part of the conflict and the space that is in between them and in which they are floating.

Step III: Allow yourself to feel each part of the conflict, by merging with each part-(icle).

Step IV: Merge with each shape, and then step between each side of the conflict and merge with the space.

Step V: See the two part-(icles) (the conflicted parts) that are floating in space and the space that surrounds them as being made of the same substance.

Step VI: Notice what happens.

● ●

One student said, "The conflict disappeared." Another student said, "The conflict lost its charge." A third student said, "The opposition disappeared: I feel calm and peaceful like it's no issue anymore."

I responded to all three of the workshop participants by stating a simple principle.

Principle: In order to have an experience or to experience anything, there must be a *contrast*, or something different from something else. To repeat Bentov again,

> "Our whole reality is constructed by constantly making such comparisons. Our senses which describe our reality to us are making these comparisons all the time. Unfortunately, our senses, having no absolute reference line, must generate their own relative reference line. But whenever we perceive something, we always perceive differences only, whether it be heat or cold, light or darkness, quiet or noisy, always compared to relative quantities. We have no absolute measure of anything, so far as our daily reality is concerned." (Bentov, 1977:22)

What this means is that if everything is made of the same substance, there can be no conflict. Why? Because, it is only when something is imagined to be different than something else that a conflict can exist.

> "*Particles are merely local condensations of the field.* Einstein said, We may therefore regard matter as being constituted by the regions of space in which the field is extremely intense. There is no place in this new kind of physics, both for the field and matter, for the field is only the matter." (Capek, 1961:319).

The next question then is, how does this condensation occur? To answer this let us move on to the next exercise.

Quantum Exercise 50

• •

Step I: Notice a conflict you are having, i.e., to stay in a relationship, to not stay in a relationship.

Step II: Notice the shape and size of each part of the conflict and the space that surrounds them and is in between them.

Step III: Allow yourself to feel each part of the conflict.

Step IV: Merge with each shape, and then step between each side of the conflict and merge with the space.

Step V: See the two particles that are floating in empty space and the empty space as being made of the same substance.

Step VI: Notice the emptiness that is left.

Step VII: Condense the emptiness and make particle 1, "should I stay in this relationship," and condense some more emptiness and make particle 2, "I should *not* stay in this relationship."

Step VIII: Now, thin out these two particles and make them back into emptiness.

Step IV: Condense emptiness making it into the parts in conflict and thin them out making them back into emptiness several times.

• •

Seeing the part-(icles) and the empty space as being the same, students have commented that the part-(icles) or conflict disappear. Why? Because there are *no contrasts*. Now, by the quantum field or emptiness condensing down and making a part-(icle) such as, "I want a relationship," and then condensing itself down more and making another part-(icle) called "I don't want a relationship," two part-icles are created that you are imagining are separate and different substances than the space which surrounds them and the quantum field or emptiness they are made from. It would be like if everything were made of snow (emptiness), and you made two snowballs (part-(icles) and put them in snow, (emptiness). Then you thinned out the snowballs and made them back into snow and did this several times, making snowballs (condensed emptiness) and thinning them back into snow, (emptiness). Another metaphor would be taking water and freezing it into ice. The emptiness is the water. The ice makes the two part-(icles), "I want a relationship" and "I don't want a relationship." Are the ice and the water different? Both are water. One is simply frozen water. They are the same substance. In the same way, the emptiness is the water and the ice, frozen emptiness, is the part-(icles), "I want a relationship" and "I don't want a relationship."

If we can view with a "quantum lens" the particles and the empty space, and the snow and snowballs, as not separate and distinct the conflict cannot exist. The conflict can only exist, if we imagine and see contrasts.

> "In the same way, the Buddhists express the same idea when they call the ultimate reality *sunnyata* for emptiness or void and affirm that it is a *living* void which gives birth to all forms in the phenomenological world." (Capra, 1976:198)

Here the living void is the same as the quantum field. The quantum field being the fundamental substance. Einstein stated, "Particles are only local condensations of the fields." Quantum Psychology would say I-dentities, subpersonalities, false selves, etc., are only local condensations of the quantum field or void. This is very profound, because here we are saying that everything is made of this quantum field or void. Everything you call yourself is a condensation of this quantum field or void.

What has occurred in quantum physics is that as we break down matter into smaller and smaller parts, eventually parts disappear and we are left with this basic Quantum field or void. Now, since everything is interconnected and disappears upon investigation, the question emerges, "If I investigate this illusive self I call "me", might it not disappear along with the problems of the self?"

In modern psychology the self is emphasized as if it existed independently. Psychology's basic goal is to create some kind of idealized self, a self that is self-actualized, according to Abraham Maslow. A self that is fully functioning.

I once worked with a transactional analysis trainer who defined health as "saying what you mean, meaning what you say, getting what you want, wanting what you get." Again we are trying to build in a self or create a self who can handle all kinds of situations and has all resources available. We are trying to create a self by imagining a "separate self" existing independently from other selves. At an implicate level, this separation is imaginary, because the self is a part-(icle) which occurs when the quantum field or emptiness condenses. This means that the self is condensed emptiness and emptiness is a thinned-out self.

Applications

Often I am asked in workshops, "How can I apply this to my real life problems?"

In 1985, I realized that I was an incest survivor, having been molested by my aunt at an early age. When I went back into therapy as a client many memories of what occurred were being held in my body as a body memory.

Many forms of body centered therapy concur, that the physical body has a memory of traumatic events. Wilhelm Reich, the grandfather of body centered therapy, wrote a detailed book entitled *Character Analysis* in the 1940s. Here Reich designates certain styles of holding our body indicating particular strategies or ways of being, perceiving and experiencing life. The body carries memories of traumatic events, consequently, with clients I work with and psychotherapists I train, I suggest that people suffering from trauma need some form of body therapy, so that the memories and traumas kept within the body can be released.

In cases of severe abuse, a simple massage can be therapeutic for the individual suffering from post traumatic stress disorder since often there is resistance to touch. Further along, Feldenkrais' "Awareness through movement"., and the body work of Rolfing have helped incest survivors "stand" in the world in a different way.

For myself, during deep tissue therapy, particularly while areas between my legs were being worked on, I quite spontaneously, saw images of my aunt's face in my mind's eye. The images of her face looked like a film; the picture would arise within that empty-space I had with my eyes closed. I began to "see" that the picture was made of the same substance as the space that surrounded the picture. I would watch the picture arise in space and be with and experience the picture of my aunt. The picture of my aunt (foreground), as I experienced it, would thin out and become the emptiness which surrounded it (background). The picture was condensed emptiness. The emptiness was thinned out picture—it was all made of the same quantum field or void.

This would later become the quantum exercise I used with numerous clients working with incest, rapes and post traumatic stress disorder. The memory of the trauma is contained within a space and is surrounded by space. After working with the memory, which is quite solid, modern psychotherapy helps the client to reduce charge from the memory, so it becomes less solid, and the client can let go of it or be less affected by the memory. As therapists know, as the issue (memory) is worked on it becomes less charged, more diffused, and the client feels freer of it. Why? Because its mass (solidness) begins to dissolve as it is experienced. At this point, whether working with your own memories or helping another with his/her past remembrances, ask the client or yourself to condense down the emptiness seen behind closed eyes and make a memory (picture), then to thin it out into the emptiness. Doing this several times helps to "see" the memory for what it is, condensed emptiness.

If you, or a client feels the picture is too solid, then have them make many *duplicate* copies of the picture (condensed emptiness) until some of the energy associated with the memory dissipates. I am not suggesting in anyway that this is the *cure all* for post traumatic stress or just burdensome unpleasant memories. This will not necessarily help everybody. This way of working can, however, be an add-on to whatever process or work that is being done. Furthermore, issues of severe trauma that carry intense emotional charge are not going to be released until the person is willing to experience the emotions involved in the trauma, to varying degrees. This approach can be used at the right moment to speed-up the letting go process. I am mentioning this, because often people have a tendency to "beat themselves up" if the memory keeps coming back. If the memory keeps coming back, the pictures and incidents still have too much energy associated with them. They must be de-solidified through experiencing, *before* they can go through this condensing-thinning out process. This approach can, in many instances help to process the problem (memory) and return it to its original substance, the quantum field or emptiness.

"The solution of the problems of life is seen in the vanishing of the problem." (Wittgenstien, 1961:73).

The next exercise will help to exemplify this.

Quantum Exercise 51

● ●

(Eyes closed)

Step I: Allow a painful memory to come up into the emptiness behind your eyes.

Step II: Be with and experience the picture.

Step III: Notice the emptiness that surrounds the picture.

Step IV: See the picture as condensed emptiness.

Step V: Condense emptiness and make it into the picture.

Step VI: Thin out the picture and make it into condensed emptiness several times, until the charge on the picture feels neutralized.

Step VII: Realize who did all of the condensing and thinning out of emptiness.

• •

Step VII is very important, because as you realize that you are condensing emptiness into a picture or memory in present time, you can stop condensing it.

Principle: Once the quantum field or emptiness condenses itself down, an experience and an experiencer are formed.

To understand this more completely in Quantum Psychology, imagine you have a memory of Dad doing something bad to you: Dad and the little boy/girl are not here in present time, i.e., Dad is not in the room. The picture (condensed emptiness) is being held by you, the observer, in present time. From a Quantum Psychology perspective, in order for you to let go of an unpleasant event or situation that is being held in the quantum field, you must experience that *you* are holding the memory there. In modern psychology, the story or picture has the power, as if it had a life of its own. Without blame or shame, a goal of Quantum Psychology is for you to experience that you are holding and condensing emptiness into a picture or memory. When this is *experienced*, you can stop organizing emptiness into a memory, which allows the condensed emptiness to go back to its original form, which is emptiness or the quantum field.

Repeat the process and ask yourself, "Who is making the emptiness condense into part-(icles) (memory), and who is making the memory (part-icles) thin out and be emptiness?" Or stated another way, once you have ice (the picture) and realize that you froze the water (emptiness), you can stop freezing the water into ice. What happens? It goes back to water (its original form).

Once again, I need to emphasize that there is no blame nor shame in what local condensations (memories) have emerged in the quantum field (emptiness). Our intention is to merely "see" them with a *quantum lens* with no judgement nor evaluation attached. This does not mean judgement and evaluation are bad and you should "get on your own case" if they are present. There are no "shoulds" involved with this. The suggestion is to see the judging part-(icle) as condensed emptiness too.

I hope you know that it's *you* who is condensing and thinning out the quantum field. Hence, you are beyond the conflict and the observer/creator and organizer of emptiness becoming form and form becoming emptiness.

> When we magnify our physical matter very much, we find that we are made mostly of void, permeated by oscillating fields. This is what objective physical reality is composed of (Bentov, 1977).

Parallel Universes

Probably, one of the most amazing theories in quantum physics, is what Nick Herbert in his book *Quantum Reality* calls,

> "Quantum Reality # 4: the many worlds interpretation (reality consists of a steadily increasing number of parallel universes.)" Of all the claims, "says Herbert, none is more outrageous than the contention that myriads of universes are created upon occasion of each measurement act." (Herbert, 1985:19).

What does this mean in light of what we have been discussing throughout the book.

Let us begin by reviewing our earlier premises.

In Chapter V, we saw that *you* as an observer created your subjective experience through the vehicle of belief and labels. In Chapters VI, VII, and VIII, we got to appreciate that the world is David Bohms' unfolding and enfolding of energy, space, mass, and time. As we move through our journey the components of energy, space, mass, and time are viewed as made of the same substance, or condensations in the Quantum field, or emptiness.

In Chapter V, we understood that we create that which we

observe. But in Chapter VIII the space that surrounds the part-(icle) or what I call the I-dentity, since it is what you call "I", are seen as the same. This causes the part-(icle) to go back to the same substance emptiness. Why? Well, as we explained earlier, you could only have an experience if there were a contrast, or one part-(icle), like, "I love myself," viewed as separate from another part-(icle), "I hate myself," and both as being separate from the space that surrounds them. If there were no contrast (this is different from that), there would be no separation, hence, no experience.

***Principle*:** All experiences require an explicate view of separation and contrasts. As soon as the contrasts are seen as local condensations in the quantum field, (created reality), the structure or distinction between energy, space, mass, and time de-constructs, goes back to its deconstructed substance, emptiness.

Simply put, we can say that part-(icles), beliefs, or I-dentities are constructed or condensed emptiness; and that emptiness is de-constructed or thinned-out part-(icles), beliefs or I-dentities.

How does this apply to the parallel universe theory that all universes exist side by side? To answer this, let us look at some major and minor approaches to self-help and enlightenment in both psychology and Eastern traditions.

Psychology

In psychology, the brilliant work of Carl Jung, M.D. demonstrated a belief structure, part-(icle) floating in emptiness, or local condensation of the quantum field. The Gestalt therapy of Fritz Perls, M.D., as well as the psychotherapy and hypnotic approach of Milton H. Erickson, M.D., were both local condensations in the quantum field. In other words, boundaried belief systems, which are condensed emptiness.

Each of the above mentioned theorists have helped countless people in their search to handle psychic pain. Each system, however, is a belief structure, and, hence, has boundaries and is composed of energy, space, mass, and time. What is meant by this can be seen in illustration #11.

Each one of these universes was a *created* structure. For

Illustration 11

Below are three different models of psychotherapy. Each model has energy, occupies space, has mass, and exists in time. Notice, however, that the emptiness that surrounds the bubble and the bubble are made of the same substance. Stated another way, the bubble is made of a condensed emptiness, or a local condensation in the Quantum field.

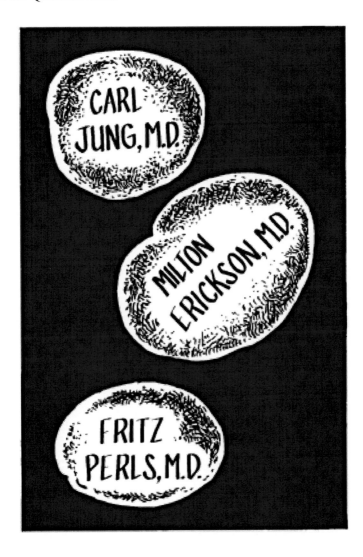

example, when I was a client in Gestalt therapy in the early 70's, Gestalt, by its disciples was viewed as the way, the truth, and the light. It was a beautiful belief structure that believed that resolving unfinished business from the past would alleviate present-time emotional pain. In many cases it worked to help people handle emotional pain. In the part-(icle) bubble of Erickson, the same is true, a belief structure that held that problems could be solved through reassociation, reframing, resource retrieval, etc. Once again, a powerful universe or *part*-(icle) bubble to enter.

The extraordinary cosmology of Jung had a part-(icle) bubble that helped people understand themselves in a new context to include their relationship to the universe, archtypes, etc.

Each one of these pioneers, and many, many others, have developed systems and structures that have helped countless people over the last so many years. I am not in any way "putting down," these systems. They are local condensations in the Quantum field.

Religious Systems

Let us now look at the Eastern and Middle Eastern philosophies of yoga, Buddhism, the Sufi tradition, and even, dare I say it, Christianity.

Since countless volumes have been written on each of these traditions, let me say for now that each tradition holds certain belief structures. Each structure, because it has never been questioned or seen as a belief, but rather is seen as the ultimate reality, can cause the practitioner to remain stuck in a separate boundaried part-(icle), a bubble like structure. To illustrate this imagine your bathtub filled with water (emptiness), and bubbles (condensed or constructed emptiness). Each bubble could be seen to represent a belief system and parallel universe (condensed emptiness). Within each parallel bubble-universe is contained a belief system, a boundary which is surrounded by the water in the tub (emptiness).

Therefore, each universe exists side by side, surrounded by the same substance or emptiness and made of the *same* quantum field. Hence, the parallel universe theory.

"Not only do space and time form a unity called spacetime, but matter is also connected to it. It's like a gigantic sponge cake. The bubbles of spacetime enclosed in the cake are meaningless without the spongy cake surrounding them. You can't have spacetime without matter, one defines the other, and vice versa." (Wolf, 1988:109)

This means, that since everything is made of the same quantum field (emptiness), then all universes exist side by side. Also, this validates Nick Herbert's *Quantum Reality #8*: "The world consists of potentials and actualities." (Herbert, 1985:26).

Here we see no contradiction between the parallel universe theory, (universes exist side by side), the world as potentials and actualities, and Nick Herbert's *Quantum Reality #7*: Consciousness Creates Reality. How can these apparent contradictory notions be reconciled. Again, if everything comes from and is made of the same quantum emptiness, then all universes exist and are paradoxically in potential. Furthermore, what is consciousness? Condensed emptiness. Therefore, consciousness creates reality. (This will be discussed more fully in Chapter XI).

Suffice it to say, for now, as soon as an undifferentiated consciousness (emptiness) is defined and labeled a part-(icle) or belief system (bubble) emerges (condensed emptiness). And, as soon as the part-(icle) is seen as being made of the same substance as all other part-(icles), conflicts cease. Why? Because no construction or imagined separation, no imagined conflicts. This can be seen in illustration #12.

Now, what do all these systems have in common?

First, they are all created.

Second, they are all beliefs.

Third, they all have energy, have solidness or mass, exist in time, and occupy a space.

Fourth, each structure is made of the same basic substance: undifferentiated consciousness, which is the quantum field.

Now, how can we put this in the light of quantum physics in general, and parallel universe theory in particular.

Parallel universe theory was invented by Hugh Everett in 1957 at Princeton University.

"Despite its bizarre conclusion, that innumerable parallel universes each as real as its own actually exist, Everett's,

Illustration 12

Below the black is the emptiness or the Quantum field. The bubbles are local condensations in the Quantum field, which we call a "spiritual path."

many-worlds picture has gained considerable support among quantum theorists." (Herbert, 1985:19)

Four questions emerge regarding this theory. First of all, how can we suggest that all universes do exist. Two, how can this apply to psychological theory. Three, how much does this help us in our own struggle to resolve conflicts. And four, where does this leave us as we journey through Quantum Psychology in our discovery of who we are.

Let us begin with the first assumption in parallel universe theory, namely that all universes exist side by side.

To do this let us take a moment to experience an exercise.

Quantum Exercise 52

• •

Step I: Let your eyes close and notice the emptiness in front of you.

Step II: Take some emptiness and condense it down and create a psychological system, like Gestalt, Jungian, Ericksonian, transactional analysis, Psychosynthesis, Freudian Analysis, etc.

Step III: Take some more emptiness and condense it down and create another psychological system.

Step IV: Condense down some more emptiness and create another psychological system.

Step V: Condense some emptiness down and create an enlightenment system, (like Yoga, Meditation, Buddhism, Sufism, Zen, Christianity, Judaism, Shamanism, Course in Miracles, Metaphysics, The Occult, etc.)

Step VI: Condense down some more emptiness and make it into another system.

Step VII: Now, step back and notice how each system appears like a bubble floating in emptiness.

● ●

This is Quantum Psychology's answer to parallel universe theory, namely that each universe actually exists side by side. Of course, one could argue that what about a system that isn't mentioned. The answer is clear, however, since the space that surrounds the bubbles, and the bubbles, are made of the same material, so all universes exist and are made of the same emptiness.

Since, as Einstein pointed out, "Everything is made of emptiness and form is condensed emptiness," then every universe exists because all are made of the same material.

This brings us back to the old idea in Buddhism of a middle path. Many teachers have suggested that the middle path means moderate eating, moderate sleeping, etc. In the purist form of Buddhism, the middle path means nothing is true, nothing is false. How does this apply? Look again at all the universes (Gestalt, Jung, Yoga, etc.) you created out of the emptiness that you saw with your eyes closed. Notice that the bubble is made of the same substance as the emptiness surrounding it. Notice the bubble de-constructs when the emptiness and the bubble are seen as the same substance.

Principle: The nothing (emptiness) contracts and becomes what would be called truth, and the nothing (emptiness) contracts and becomes what is called false. In short, the nothing (emptiness) becomes truth, the nothing (emptiness) becomes false.

Presently, there is a New Age comedian who calls himself Swami Beyondananda. He has said, "People that have been working on themselves, doing spiritual disciplines and psychological studies, deserve NOTHING. If you've tried so many paths, I can say with confidence NOTHING WORKS." Here Einstein, Buddha and Beyondananda concur; form is contracted emptiness, emptiness is form. Therefore, seekers deserve NOTHING.

How the parallel universe theory applies to Quantum Psychology and to our lives becomes clearer as we continue on our experiential journey.

Quantum Exercise 53

• •

Step I: Let your eyes close and notice the emptiness in front of you.

Step II: Take some emptiness and condense it down and create a psychological system, like Gestalt or Jungian or Ericksonian or Transactional Analysis or Psychosynthesis or Freudian Analysis, etc.

Step III: Take some more emptiness and condense it down and create another psychological system.

Step IV: Condense down some more emptiness and create another psychological system.

Step V: Condense some emptiness down and create an enlightenment system, like Yoga, Meditation, Shamanism, Course in Miracles, Buddhism, Sufism, Zen, Christianity, Judaism.

Step VI: Condense down some more emptiness and make it into another system.

Step VII: Now, step back and notice how each system appears like a bubble floating in space.

Step VIII: Now, merge with each belief system one by one, and notice how when you are in one belief system (bubble), you experience that system to the exclusion of the others. Move from one to the next experiencing each bubble, than "pop-out" and witness each one.

Step IX: Notice who did all of that (made emptiness into form) (or thinned out form to make it into emptiness).

● ●

Finally, how does this apply to our own lives? Any conflict, either within myself or that which appears outside of myself, requires that I merge with a part-(icle) (bubble) and imagine it is separate from another part-icle (bubble).

When something is in your consciousness, like anger, for example, the anger, when seen as a part-(icle) or as a wave (see Chapter III), and, also, when the space surrounding this part-(icle) of anger is seen as the same substance, the anger loses its contrast*ness*, and cannot be held in consciousness so easily.

Let us see now how this can be applied to relationships.

The Relationship Process

The purpose of the relationship process is to see conflicts in a relationship as part-(icles), or bubbles in opposition that are floating in emptiness. As mentioned earlier, nothing can be experienced unless there is a contrast, or we could say nothing can be experienced if there is no contrast. Form and emptiness, day and night, black and white, love and hate, feeling and no feeling, cold and hot—everything has its opposite. Without a contrast, there could be no experiences. In a relationship, the only way there can be an argument or a fight, is if there are two opposing part-(icles) or bubbles.

In order for you to have a fight, argument, or a disagreement with your relationship, whether it be your partner, wife, mother, husband, daughter, whoever, you have to identify yourself as a particular position or part-(icle) in emptiness. Whoever that person is that you are arguing with, also has to be identified with a particular opposing bubble or part-(icle), held in emptiness.

Quantum Exercise 54

● ●

Step I: Notice when you are in a conflict with anyone.

Step II: Step outside of, and witness or observe the belief system bubble that you are identifying with. For example, if you want something and your partner does not, experience the wanting, notice its size and shape, see it as energy.

Step III: Notice the difference between you and this part-(icle).

Step IV: Notice the space surrounding the part-(icle).

Step V: Notice the opposite part-(icle) called "husband" or "wife" and its size and shape. Do this until you can see both part-(icles) as energy floating in emptiness.

Step VI: Be part-(icle), bubble or position A and look at position B.

Step VII: Be part-(icle), bubble or position B and look at position A.

Step VIII: Be the emptiness and look at both part-(icle) bubble A and part-(icle) bubble B.

Step IX: See the two part-(icles) that are positions as made of the same substance as the emptiness surrounding them.

Step X: Allow them to deconstruct since there is no contrast.

Step XI: Practice condensing and thinning-out emptiness into part-(icles) and part-(icles) into emptiness.

Step XII: Turn your attention around. Notice who did all of that.

● ●

So, the first thing you have to do, is to not be identified with your position or be identified with the oppositional position, called "husband". Let's say, for example, you want to go out and your husband wants to stay in. You get into a huge fight and you're saying, "I want to go, we never go out," and so on. He says, "I want to stay in." Obviously you both are identified with two particular part-(icles) or bubbles.

As soon as the part-(icles) and the space are seen as the same, de-construction occurs and they disappear. *No contrasts.*

This process has brought several mixed reactions from workshop participants. One woman said, "It was not difficult being my husband's bubble, but when I took on and experienced my daughter's part-(icle), it was overwhelmingly painful."

I replied, "Until you can be free to experience, and free not to experience, your daughter's position, you can not pop-out of the part-(icle) and observe it so that it de-constructs."

Another man said, "I felt freer and it helped me to appreciate my wife's position." "Generally," I replied, "You have to keep playing with taking on and taking off the positions—like putting on and taking off a shirt—until, the opposing position charge is diminished enough so that you can just observe the part-(icle) bubble in emptiness with no judgment, evaluation, or significance attached to the opposing position."

Common Questions

A student asked, "Where does this part-(icle) go?" I replied, "When there is no contrast, there is no conflict, so it de-constructs or de-condenses." The local condensation of the quantum field stops condensing. It is not that it disappears, but it changes back to its decondensed nature, which is the quantum field or emptiness."

Another student said, "My part-(icle) was about being angry with my husband because he doesn't give me what I want. My feelings and position on that didn't change and didn't disappear. What should I do?"

I said, "first of all you are going to have to go back and *feel* and *experience* your feelings of wanting. Secondly, I would recommend creating the feelings of wanting again, and again, and again until you can witness or observe that feeling. Next, you will have to be willing to *have* the anger or *not have* the anger. What I mean is, that if you do these exercises to get rid of something, you are resisting the feelings you are trying to get rid of. You have to be able to be *free to have or free to not have the feelings*. Then, when you see the feelings and the space as being made of the same substance, you can notice or be interested in what happens. "Notice" and "interested" are the important words. You could even use the word "curious", while allowing *whatever* to happen when the feeling is viewed as the same as the emptiness surrounding it. Remember, (as mentioned in Chapter IV) these exercises are done with *no intention*.

This does not mean that you should give up what you want from your husband. It does mean, however, that when you develop the ability to observe the emptiness organizing into form and form moving back to emptiness, the choice of what to do or not to do in regard to your relationship will become clearer.

The Physical Body

One other thing needs to be noted. The physical body has particular, organic, biological functioning. To put it more bluntly, I'll quote an Indian teacher of mine who said, "All our time is spent eating, sleeping, shitting, and fucking, or how to make more money so you have a better place to do it in." *Bodily responses are not processible.* The body needs to eat, sleep, shit and fuck. Problems arise when sex becomes a substitute for feeling a lack of love, or food becomes a substitute for security or comfort. Sleep or tiredness can be a depression or a way of resisting feeling. This process, whereby, an individual sublimates or substitutes food for a lack of self-esteem is *processible.* Quantum Psychology does not, like many spiritual disciplines, talk about abstinence or resisting a bodily function like food, sex, or sleep. Rather, Quantum Psychology suggests that the sublimation or substitution of wanting love for food as a *compulsion* can be de-constructed by recognizing its origin, the emptiness. The bodily functions will continue, while the self-defeating tendency of sublimation leaves people not feeling free or getting what they *really* want. It is the resistance to a bodily function, or abstinence, that causes problems. Why? Because it is labeled as "unholy" or "not godly" to feel sexual. It is something to be resisted. Those feelings must be kept there so that you can always know what you're not suppose to have. Furthermore, it causes sublimation or substitution.

Noted psychiatrist Dr. Wilhelm Reich suggests further that abstinence from sexual orgasm closes the natural ability the body has to discharge energy. This energy, rather than going out through the genitals, must go somewhere. Where does it go? Reich suggests that the energy moves upward toward the head, causing more thoughts. Consequently, the sexual abstinence, professed by Eastern spiritual disciplines to promote a "quite, calm, peaceful" mind, might yield opposite results. Certainly, this was true in my case because the energy did not go out but went to my head and into more thoughts.

Furthermore, Reich suggests strongly that forced sexual abstinence (celibacy) forces the energy upward into fantasy causing the fantasized *mystification* of the world. This is why members of the celibate, spiritual community, I was involved with, along with myself, tended to mystify everything into the fantasy of gods and goddesses as part of the "magical thinking" of our daily experiences. This would also explain the mystification of the teachers or guru. Imposed celibacy in the community I lived in caused mystification of the "power" of the man or woman Guru. Often times devotees would project such magical qualities onto the teacher making statements like, "he knows exactly what I need," or he knows my every thought or desire." This "magical" mystification of a teacher can be traced back to age-regressed childhood states, where Mommy and Daddy are responsible for you and many times stayed vigilant to fulfill your needs.*

Often times, parents will say, "if you need it, I'll give it to you." The child takes this idealized and spiritualized parent and projects it on the guru or god. Children believe that pleasing the parent gets them what they need from the parent; this too is projected on the outer teacher or god.

Parallels between pleasing the guru, or God, and pleasing Mom and Dad can be drawn. The co-dependence or necessary dependence of the child on the parents for survival can carry through in an age-regressed ego state within the adult, as he/she projects his/her Mommy and Daddy on an "idealized" teacher. In the middle seventies, I used to call this process "transpersonal transference", whereby god, Guru, or teacher is attributed magical powers by the adult/child. The paths, so often given as the only solution, are simply parent to child trances. For example, a child is told, "if you're good, you'll get love." The mystified teacher/projected idealized parent says, "be good, follow my rules, and you'll get liberation, bliss, love, etc. My father's enlightenment was a house in the suburbs and two kids. Many teacher's heaven is ... fill in the blanks. I mention this because Quantum Psychology does not claim to be the only way.

Quantum Psychology does not suggest good or bad. While in an Indian monastery my friends and I were always waiting for the "divine meat axe" for doing something we should not be doing or thinking, just as in my house as a child. One teacher said people are much smarter than God. People know all about good and bad, right and wrong, high and low, sin and virtue. God doesn't know anything about these. GOD JUST IS."

One workshop participant said, "I am left with nothing. I feel empty and a little depressed."

I read a quote from noted physicist John Wheeler.

"The nothingness of space can be seen as composed of fundamental building blocks. If we could examine it microscopically we would find that the fabric of space-time or

---

*This trance of spiritualization is discussed in depth in *The Trances of the Inner Child: The Dark Side*, Chapter 14. Bramble Books, Publication date: Fall 1993.

'superspace' is composed of a turbulent sea of bubbles."
(DeWitt and Wheeler, 1968)

This can further be appreciated in the context of Chinese Philosophy and more specifically Taoism. The Chinese use the word Chi to denote the basic energy emanating from this living breathing emptiness. Chi can condense into objects or thin-out into emptiness.

> "When the Chi condenses, its visibility becomes apparent so that there are then the shapes of individual things, when it disperses, its visibility is no longer apparent and there are no shapes. The Great Void cannot but consist of Chi; this Chi cannot but condense to form all things; and these things cannot but become dispersed, so as to form (once more) the Great Void." (Fung,1958:279-228)

In terms of physics, Wheeler says these bubbles are the warp and weft of empty space and comprise, what Wheeler calls, the "Quantum foam." He states, "The space of quantum geometro-dynamics can be compared to a carpet of foam spread over a slowly undulating landscape"...The continual microscopic changes in the carpet of foam, as new bubbles appear and old ones disappear, symbolize the quantum fluctuations in geometry." (DeWitt and Wheeler, 1968).

This understanding in physics must be experienced and known directly, however. The purpose of the exercises and all the trainings and seminars we give called Quantum Psychology® is not to add another belief system, but rather to make available approaches that provide an experiential knowingness of what physics has already proven.

Furthermore, the bubbles mentioned by Wheeler are likened to, and similar to, the part-(icles) or I-dentities. Often people in workshops experience these I-dentities as bubbles floating in emptiness. Once the emptiness and the bubble or part-(icle) are seen as the same, the nothingness or what Wheeler calls the "building block" of existence remains. The nothing becomes a something (when condensed), the something (condensed nothing) becomes nothing when thinned-out or de-constructed. This is talked about by Lama Goumda,

"The relationship of form and emptiness cannot be con-
ceived as a state of mutually exclusive opposites, but only
as two aspects of the same reality, which coexist and are in
continual cooperation." (Govinda, 1974:223)

What Wheeler says is, "nothingness is the building blocks of
the universe." The emptiness is made of the same substance as particles be it a feeling or thought or emotion, etc. They are all one and
the same. Now to go back to the comment, "I feel empty and
depressed." People put judgements, evaluations, and decisions on
what the experience of emptiness means, like it is "not good" or it
means "I'm empty or depressed." These are *labels* that are tacked
on to pure emptiness. Without a judgment or decision as to what the
emptiness means, only ISNESS remains .

Recently, I was working with a client who was continually
trying to fill up the empty void she felt inside, she labeled it
"unwanted". By trying to fill up this empty void, she was resisting
that empty space. As we began to "do therapy," she began to
experience that the emptiness was always there and it was what
everything came from and went back to. In her words, "My whole
perception has changed. I feel comfortable and at peace." A week
later she said, "Where were you twenty years ago when I was taking
drugs. This is better than drugs." Another client complained of
compulsive over-eating. I saw that she was resisting emptiness and
was trying to "fill it up" with food. This is very common for over-
eaters, the resistance to emptiness. Interestingly enough, Buddhists
often say that our greatest resistance is to "nothing."*

If you are feeling the emptiness is "not okay," then notice the
label or judgment you have about it, and realize that it is just a label,
not who you really are. Then see the label and the part-icle and the
emptiness as made of the same substance.

The other day, I was working with a depressed man. I asked
him, "How do you experience the depression?" He said, "As empty,
void, nothingness." The client labeled the void as depression. A
week later a Buddhist friend of mine said, "I just want to experience
the bliss of the VOID." He labeled the void as bliss. I laughed
because I realized that half of the people I know are trying to get into

---

*This will be discussed in my next book, *The Tao of Chaos: Quantum Consciousness Vol.
II.*, i.e., the personality types of the enneagram organizes around essence in the body.

the void, the other half are trying to get out of the void. *It's all in the labeling.*

Another workshop participant said, "What about enlightenment?" I replied by saying, "In Buddhist terms, the ultimate is called Nirvana, and *this* world is called samsara. Buddha realized, that since the emptiness was the same as the form that surrounds us, or as Einstein said, "Everything is emptiness and form is condensed emptiness," then to see one as different from the other, would be to *not see* what was there. To paraphrase the Buddha, a person seeking the ultimate (Nirvana) is ignorant; a person seeking the world (samsara) is ignorant.

Since emptiness and form are the same, then to seek one and oppose the other, would be not to understand the nature of the universe; or to see only the explicate order of separation and not the implicate or quantum unity. This leads to Buddha's historic statement,

> "Nirvana (the ultimate) is samsara,
> Samsara (the world) is nirvana."

Whittaker, a noted physicist says it this way,

> "In Einstein's conception, space is no longer the stage on which the drama of physics is performed; it is itself one of the performers." (Whittaker, 1948)

Where then does that leave enlightenment? Possibly, it is just another concept surrounded by emptiness.

Finally, one student remarked, "This leaves me with no model, nothing to find out who I am."

I responded by quoting an Indian teacher I worked with: "In order to find out who you are, I must liken it to a pole vaulter going over the bar, in order to go over to the other side, you must let go of the pole, in the same way, you must let go of your concepts and models of reality."

This leads us into the next chapter. Now that we have the emptiness in front of us, *who are we?*

NINE

GOING BEYOND ORDINARY REALITY

Thus far we have moved from witness to creator and from creator to its relationship to energy, space, mass, and time. In this chapter we will deal with (1) getting beyond the observer/creator of experience and (2) the discovery that the observer/creator and its creation, (the part-(icle)) I-dentity called, "I hate myself", or the part-(icle) I-dentity called "I love myself", "I am angry", etc.) is made of the same essential substance as the observer.

But for now first things first: the experience that you are beyond the creator/observer.

Level 7

The observer is the observed.

Quantum Exercise 55

● ●

To be done in pairs.

Before doing exercises, we should probably s-t-r-e-c-t-h our Quantum muscles to warm-up.

Quantum warm-up stretches: going beyond the observer who creates reality.

Break down into groups of two. One person designates himself as Person A, the other as Person B. Person A faces Person B.

1. **Person A asks: Tell me a difference between you and your mind.**

   Person B: responds. (Keep asking for ten minutes.) Then change sides and Person B will ask the same question of Person A.

(Reverse)

2. **Person B: Tell me a difference between you and your body.**

   Person A: responds.

(Reverse)

3. **Person A: Tell me a difference between you and awareness.**

   Person B: responds.

   (Here, awareness is used to denote the medium you use to become aware of something.)

   This approach can be used in working with oneself. Let's say for example, if a thought, feeling, emotion, picture, etc. pops-up for you; by immediately asking yourself, "What is the difference between me and the thought or emotion," you can begin to observe by seeing a separation. Since you are the observer of it, it is Not You.

●●●●●●●●●●●●●●●●●●●●●●●●●●●●●●●

Quantum Exercise 56

●●●●●●●●●●●●●●●●●●●●●●●●●●●●●

To be done in pairs

The last group of exercises are warm-ups. The next jump is to move us to being aware of the observer. Since we can be *aware* of the observer and the creator, we are beyond the observer and creator. Once again, "Anything that you know about cannot be you" (Alfred Korsybski). If this could be put simply, we are asking you to be aware of being aware, or be aware of the observer.

This exercise is done in pairs. One person designates themselves person A, the other person B.

Person A: Tell me a difference between you and the observer.

Person B: Responds

After ten minutes, change sides, and person B asks, person A responds.

Person A: Tell me a difference between you and the observer of feelings.

Person B: Responds.

After ten minutes, change sides, and person B asks, person A responds.

Person A: Tell me a difference between you and the observer of thoughts.

Person B: Responds

After ten minutes, change sides, and person B asks, person A responds.

Person A: Tell me a difference between you and the observer of sensations.

Person B: Responds.

After ten minutes, change sides, and person B asks, person A responds.

● ●

This can be done until the person opposite you begins to see thoughts as part-(icles) or bubbles floating in emptiness. Each part-(icle) bubble carries with it the experience, with beliefs, ideas, storyline, and evidence to validate what it is experiencing. This, as was referred to in my earlier book, *Trances People Live: Healing Approaches in Quantum Psychology*, is a trance, because you have to become a tiny part-(icle) and shrink yourself down to a part-(icle), or point of view. This is what in psychotherapy would be called a "false self", sub-personality, a part, an I-dentity, or an ego state. The observer, too, is a trance. Why? Since you can be aware of the observer, and you can be aware of being aware, then you are more than the observer. If, however, you shrink yourself down and become an observer, you will *create* something to observe, because that is the function of the observer: to participate in the creation of that which is observed.

For example, take a belief or an experience called, "I like myself," or an experience called, "I don't like myself," and notice the shape of that particular belief. All beliefs, part-(icles) or bubbles have shapes to them, as mentioned in Chapter V. If you notice the shape, then you notice that inside the experience, or part-(icle) called, "I don't like myself," are all the situations, all the experiences, all the history that this statement, this belief has asserted. It's a tautology, which means it is self-organizing in that if you believe, "I don't like myself," then that will constantly be reinforced. This is a closed loop. The observer creates, "I don't like myself." This creates a history, with thoughts, feelings, emotions, etc. to validate its creation. In essence, the observer/creator organizes the empty space so that empty space becomes condensed and appears as a reality and true. The observer fuses with the condensed emptiness as a reality, and it becomes a closed loop (in psychological terms). In other words, everything the observer creates, reinforces everything else. To illustrate, if the observer organizes the empty space and creates, "I don't like myself," this created reality acts as a filter and interprets interaction through this *filter*. This, becomes a closed circuit:

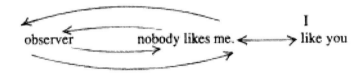

In this illustration, the closed intrapsychic loop of observer creating, "Nobody likes me," cannot allow in any other information. It can interpret the information, "I like you," as "It is not so," or by just not allowing it inside the system.

Quantum Psychology
and the New Age

The question often arises in workshops about beliefs creating external events. I have had New Agers who believe they create external events happening to them because of the beliefs they hold to be true. Quantum Psychology is very different than New Age Schools, which imagine that because I have a particular belief, *"Nobody likes me,"* that I will therefore *attract* people to me who don't like me to re-enforce my, *"Nobody likes me."* Quantum Psychology states that the belief part-(icle) *"Nobody likes me,"* acts as a filter and only creates that experience *subjectively*, whether it is there or not. Example: if, when I look at you, I believe you don't love me I will experience *"You don't love me!"* This does not mean you don't love me. It means, subjectively, I will only experience my belief and thus experience *"You don't love me!"* This is the self-organizing aspect of a part-(icle) or I-dentity. The I-dentity part-(icle) keeps itself mass-like and solid by continually perceiving reality as re-enforcing its beliefs. This is only *subjective*. I do not create *"not loving me"* in you. I only create my subjective experience of *"You don't love me!"* Hence, I create my own *subjective* reality!

In cognitive therapy this is called "mind reading." Simply put, if I believe nobody likes me, I project that you don't like me, and then I act as if this mind reading were the truth. Often times, people as children develop this "cognitive distortion" as a way to handle their parental situation. Mind-reading Mommy's or Daddy's wants could certainly help a child to please them and survive. The child learned that *mind reading* and pleasing an alcoholic or abusive parent might be a way to "keep the peace." Unfortunately, as the child becomes an adult he takes this *mind reading* with him on automatic. The adult, with this mechanism running, will *mind read*, unknowingly, the present-time situation, as if it were the threatening past.

Many clients have told me that, "Nobody likes me" or "My husband/wife doesn't love me." They *feel* that way even if friends like them or their partners act and verbally interact with love. Why? Because the observer, once they create "Nobody loves me," will filter out all else and even make "Nobody Loves me" their *subjec-*

tive reality, as mentioned in Chapter V. Once a part-(icle) I-dentity becomes that defined and solidified, no information contrary to its belief structure can get in!!!

This is very different than New Age thinkers who believe that we bring to ourselves "external" conditions to re-enforce our belief structure. We are saying in Quantum Psychology that the observer sources its own internal subjective experience, not the internal subjective experience of another. Let me give an example from the first chapter of *Trances People Live*.

> "If I say, "I like you," you may create any number of responses: (1) That's nice; (2) He didn't really mean it;" (3) "If he only knew what I was really like he wouldn't feel that way; (4) I wonder what he wants from me. (Wolinsky, 1991:3)

Here the observer is sourcing his/her internal, *subjective* responses to a particular person saying "I like you." Many New Age thinkers might say, "Why did I create that person to say, I like you," or "What lessons am I suppose to learn from them," etc. This is what we call *super-source*. Super-source is imagining that you are sourcing (creating) someone else's experience. This, of course, is an "age-regressed" position that comes from childhood. In psychological terms it would be called "infantile grandiosity," whereby the child believes it *makes* mother or father feel good or bad, or that he/she is *responsible* for Mom or Dad's experience. As a possible scenario, the baby is lying in its crib and feels cold. Mom comes and puts a blanket on. She/he wants to get picked up. Dad comes and picks the child up. She/he is hungry. Somebody comes to feed her/him. The baby decides something like, "Through my thoughts or feelings I can bring people to me to give me what I need. I create Mom/Dad coming." This, of course, is easily re-enforced by Mom/Dad saying, "You made me feel angry."

This is the food for obsessive thinking. Let's imagine that the child is hungry and several times the Mom/Dad doesn't awake to feed the child immediately. The baby thinks, "Well since my thoughts created them coming before, if I think *harder*, I can get them to come and give me what I need. Maybe I should see (visualize) them coming to me giving me what I want. This is called primary process in psychoanalytic terminology and is so basic that it overlays into many areas in our lives.

In this age-regressed grandiose state, which is a trance, people feel they are responsible for what other people feel, think or do. Although volumes have been written on co-dependence, suffice to say for now, that the observer (you) sources his/her own subjective experience, not someone else's reaction to you. Often in workshops, I'll say something like, "I have no idea how subjectively you are creating me inside yourselves. I must say however, when I gave up trying to control how other people created me in their subjective experience, I felt much freer. Because I no longer spent my energy trying to get people to see me a certain way, I was able to allow people to have whatever experience they were having of me." People have I-dentities which resist another's subjective creation. For example, a women of 45 I was working with was still "taking care" of mom who was needy and dependent. I asked her, "Are you willing to allow your mother to have her pain?" She said, "No." This is where the therapy must go. Why is her age-regressed I-dentity resisting her mothers' subjective creation of pain?

Another client, an attorney, always felt people thought he wasn't smart. The question and session dealt with his resistance to the possibility (mind-reading) that others were creating him subjectively as *"not smart."* He had a deep resistance to others' subjective creation. To over compensate he *tried* hard to *be smart*; rather than allowing other people to have their subjective experience of him.

This grandiosity leads to blaming oneself for external events, or trying to re-frame unpleasant external events into "lessons."

Quantum Psychology is suggesting an inner focus, in which you notice the observer and what he/she creates as made of the same essential substance—no blame, no lessons, no reasons, no purpose, no judgement, no evaluation or significance, no shame. Emptiness results in organizing or condensing itself into form, form de-condensing or de-constructing itself into emptiness.

The Psychology of Prior Created Part-(icle) Identities

Often in psychotherapy a new decision is offered to the client *over* the old decision. For example, if someone has decided, "Men or women are trustworthy," many forms of therapy offer the re-decision "Sometimes men/women can be trusted," or "It is okay to trust," or some facsimile thereof. This attempt to re-organize experiences by re-organizing the beliefs usually yields marginal results.

Principle: Once an observer creates a belief, the first belief is the strongest. Hence, creating a new belief over an earlier belief, causes more conflict.

It is hoped that this principle explains the partial failure of both psychology's re-decision and the New Age thinker's "thought affirmation." In both cases, the observer creates an "unwanted belief," such as, "The world isn't safe," and attempts to change the belief to, "The world is safe." Every time you write, affirm, or re-decide 'The world is safe," you are re-enforcing its opposite. You must keep the first decision there to know what you don't want.

Let's take another example. A client comes in and complains in some way about his/her inability to deal with authority. During the session, he/she says, "I didn't want to be like Mom/Dad; I decided to be the opposite." From a quantum perspective, this client must keep "Mom/Dad" in consciousness in order to always know what not to be. The first creation is an impression of "Mom/Dad," and the one created in opposition is, "I won't be like them." Two things occur. First, under stress, adults sound just like their mothers and fathers (the first created impression). Secondly, if both realities are to be held by the observer, the "Mom/Dad" can be projected on a boss, a husband, wife, or the loan officer at the bank. Another scenario might be that as a boss or authority figure a person will become just like "Mom/Dad," filtering out other information and perceiving the employee as a helpless child, the second created impression.

These, are examples of how an observer creates various bubbles and experiences of life through these structures.*

In, Quantum Exercise 55, we got clearer about the observer created reality and the difference between the observer and the observed. In Exercise 56, we are asking you to see that you are beyond the observer and the observed, or you might say we ask that

---

*The topics of oppositional identities and the grandiose nature of an age-regressed child is discussed in detail in *The Trances of the Inner Child: The Dark Side* by Stephen Wolinsky, Ph.D., Bramble Books, Publication date: Fall 1993.

you be aware of being aware. Please DO NOT GO ON TO Quantum Exercise 57 until it is very clear to you that you can *be aware* of the observer and its creation. You might even want to spend a day, a week or whatever time it takes to practice being aware of the observer. This can be done by continually asking yourself the questions in the previous exercises. "What is the difference between me and the observer of feelings, thoughts, or emotions?" If it is not experiencable stop and work with it until it is. This next Quantum jump requires the clarity of the step before it.

Quantum Exercise 57

● ●

"Everything is made of emptiness and form is condensed emptiness." (Albert Einstein)

Step I: Notice an experience, belief, or I-dentity that is troubling you, like, "I don't like myself."

Step II: Notice the shape of the part-(icle) I-dentity; this will put you outside of the part-(icle) I-dentity.

Step III: Continue to move your awareness farther out so that you notice that the part-(icle) I-dentity called, "I don't like myself," is like a bubble floating in emptiness.

Step IV: Allow the bubble that is floating in emptiness to be seen as condensed emptiness. In other words, notice that the emptiness is condensed down and made into that bubble and that if it were thinned out, it would be in emptiness.

Step V: **Notice what happens when you recognize this.**

● ●

The Observer is Made of the Same Substance as the Observed

In order to experience a problem state, one must imagine and pretend that there is a difference between the observer and that experience the observer creates. For example, if an observer creates the experience, "I like myself," the observer must pretend that it is made of a different substance than the observed. If an observer does *not* pretend that, and the substances are viewed as the same, then there can be no contrasts, therefore no experience.

Problems can only arise as long as there is an "I" separate from the problem. Once the substance, i.e., observer and observed, is seen as the same, the problem and the experiencer of the problem merge and disappear.

Quantum Exercise 58

● ●

In quantum physics, the scientists are joined in a complex system with no distinct, well-defined parts, and the experimental apparatus does not have to be described as an isolated physical entity for the scientist to include it in the scientific experiment. Another way of saying it is that *subject and object are joined ... or the subject and object only exist as one.* (Capra, 1976:121).

Step I: Notice when you are having an experience, i.e., "I love myself", anger, etc.).

Step II: Notice the observer of the experience.

Step III: Notice the difference between you and the observer by asking yourself, "What is the difference between me and the observer?"

Step IV: See the observer and its object (the ob-
            served experience) as the same substance.

Step V: Notice what happens.

● ●

Principle: Every time a problem arises, note that the problem state, the experiencer of the problem, and the problem, have no inherent self-nature; i.e., they are not separate from each other.

Buddhist literature often uses the term self-nature, that one has no inherent self nature. What this translates to is that the observer and the observed and the empty-space surrounding it are all made of the same quantum field or emptiness. In order to have a separate self, things would be required to be made of different substances.

In other words, perceive the observer of the problem and the problem to be one. Allow them to be one. When they are seen as one everything merges and loses its *contrastness*.

Since everything is interdependent and inter-penetrates everything else, there is no *independent* nature. Once this is noticed, the problem de-constructs, because there are no contrasts.

Principle: The observer and the observed are made of the same quantum field or emptiness. The observer arises with the observed simultaneously, and subsides simultaneously.

Quantum Exercise 59

● ●

The observer and observed arise and subside together.

Step I: Notice an experience.

Step II: Notice the observer of an experience.

Step III: Notice the difference between you and the
            observer.

Step IV: **Allow the observer and object (observed) to arise and subside together.**

• •

There Is Not One Observer

In order to go beyond the observer and the observed, we must understand that each I-dentity has an observer. In other words the observer and observed is a unit. It appears as though each "I" arises independent of an observer and that the same observer observes all of these different "I's". Actually, each "I" has its own observer. What are we left with when the observer-observed are seen as one unit and made of the same substance? We are left with what the famous Indian teacher Ramana Maharish; called the "I-I". In the fourth way tradition of G.I. Gurdjieff it is called "the Real I." In Quantum Psychology we call it a no-state state, where there is knowing without a knower or awareness with no object to be aware of.

Quantum Exercise Made Simple

1. Notice an I-dentity, part-(icle), or experience that is occurring.

2. Notice an observer observing the "I".

3. Ask yourself, "What observer is observing this I-dentity, part-(icle) or experience?"

4. Notice what happens.

The Appearance of the Observer

To re-state, it appears as though there is only one stable observer observing everything coming and going. There is actually an observer which arises with each event. The observer and observed arise and subside together. This subtle understanding and experience moves us beyond the observer/observed dyad into the I-I, Real I, or no-state state.

At this level we can begin to understand and appreciate that not only is the observer-observed a unit, they are made of condensed emptiness. The observer, so important in many traditions, is actually a part-(icle) I-dentity. Although it can be argued that it is a higher I-dentity than an ordinary I-dentity, it is still an I-dentity.

As we trace our path from Level 1 we can see the necessity of splitting off the personality into observer-observed. At this level, however, we can see that to be aware of the observer, or being aware of being aware, leads us to a place beyond ordinary observer-observed reality. To restate Bentov,

> "Our objective reality is composed of a void full of pulsating fields. If we stop the pulsation of the fields, we get back to the absolute." (Bentov, 1977:67)

What Bentov is suggesting here is that this process is like a pendulum. The observer and his/her experience go from the emptiness at the top of the swing to condensed emptiness. The pendulum moves, then it stops and thins-out before it condenses in its movement. Bentov suggests that this cycle occurs up to 14 times a second.

Illustration 13

Notice that emptiness condenses and thins-out like the motion of a pendulum. This can be likened to the *Spanda* or divine pulsation discussed in Chapter III, where form becomes emptiness, emptiness becomes form. This understanding is the Heart Sutra and is the heart of Buddhism.

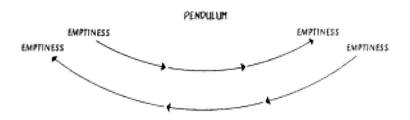

This means that whether we know it or not, we are experiencing no contrasts and quantum consciousness 14 times a second. Why don't we know it? Because without a contrast in the emptiness at the top of the swing of the pendulum, there is no "you" to observe it.

Quantum Jump

In the earlier chapters we discussed "observation creates reality." Here we will focus on yet another aspect of Quantum reality: There is no reality in the absence of observation." (Herbert, 1985:17)

Quantum Exercise 60

• •

This exercise relates back to the chapter on time. A major illusion, is that the observer was "there" observing *before* the observed or object (feeling, thought, etc.) arose. Many New Agers and practitioners of Eastern religion talk of the witness either creating or always being there, "as if you were the observer."

In Chapters III, IV and V, we are asked to be the witness or observer. Notice how the observer creates reality through the act of observation. Here, we are asked to make the "quantum jump," like a pole vaulter, and leave that stepping stone behind us. Earlier we are asked to pierce through another *illusion* of time, and realize that you as the witness or observer were there *before* the observed. In this Quantum jump we go even more deeply into the observed and the observer, not only being the same substance, but they arise and subside together.

Step I: **Notice an experience.**

Step II: **Notice the observer of an experience.**

Step III: Notice the difference between you and the observer.

Step IV: Allow the observer and object (observed) (thought or emotions, etc.) to arise and subside together.

Step V: Notice the no you—you that is present during the rising and subsiding.

•••••••••••••••••••••••••••••••••

Quantum Contemplation

If there were no "you" to be doing the observing, would you know that a problem existed?

Consider: If there were no "you" there to observe a problem, there would be nobody there to know it was a problem.

In Ken Wilber's *No Boundary* he states, "There is no boundary between subject and object, self and non-self, seer and seen." (Wilber, 1981:40).

What Wilber is saying here is exactly what this exercise is asking you to experience, that the observer and observed are the same; there is no boundary between them. Many disciplines have suggested multitudes of ways to destroy or get rid of this observer/observed boundary. Wilber states,

> "We really don't have to go to the trouble of trying to destroy the primary boundary, and for an extremely simple reason: the primary boundary doesn't exist at all." (Wilber, 1981:47)

Let me relate this back to the time I was in Santa Rosa, California in 1988. Sitting in my meditation room, I decided to look for the one that was reading quantum physics and doing all these psycho-spiritual practices for so many years. When I *turned my attention around* and tried to find the self who was doing this, I couldn't find it. *There was nothing there.* The seeker wasn't there. I realized the seeker and the *sought* are made of the same substance.

Principle: There is no thinker, only thinking.

Quantum Exercise 61

● ●

Step I: **Notice a thought passing by.**

Step II: **Turn your attention around and try to find who is thinking the thought and notice there is none.**

Step III: **Notice that there is no thinker—just thinking. *The Thinker is the Thinking.***

Step IV: **The thinker and the thinking are one, hence, no thinker.**

● ●

Principle: There is no feeler.

Quantum Exercise 62

● ●

Step I: **Notice a feeling.**

Step II: **Turn your attention around and try to find who is feeling the feeling, and notice there is just feeling with no feeler.**

Step III: **Notice that there is no "you" feeling, just feeling.**

Step IV: **The feeler is the feeling, hence, there is no feeler.**

● ●

Principle: There is no sensor.

Quantum Exercise 63

• •

Step I: **Notice a sensation.**

Step II: **Turn your attention around and try to find who is sensing the sensation, and notice the sensor is the sensation of sensing.**

Step III: **Notice that there is no "you" sensing, just sensation sensing.**

Step IV: **The sensor is the sensation, hence, no sensor.**

• •

Quantum Exercise 64

• •

Step I: **Notice an emotion.**

Step II: **Turn your attention around and try to find who is having emotions, and notice there is just emotions, with no person having the emotions.**

Step III: **Notice that there is no "you" having emotions.**

Step IV: **The "emotioner" is the emotion, hence, no emotioner.**

• •

Principle: There is no person having associations, just associations
Principle: There is no hearer, just hearing.

Quantum Exercise 65

● ●

Step I: Notice hearing.

Step II: Turn your attention around and try to find who is hearing, and notice there is just hearing with no hearer.

Step III: Notice that the hearing and hearer are one, hence, no hearer.

● ●

It becomes quite obvious that there is no individual self, just feeling, hearing, thinking.

Principle: Once conceptual ideas or beliefs are de-constructed, what is left is "isness."

Quantum Exercise 66

● ●

Step I: Look at an object. Pull your attention away from the object, going inward past all concepts or knowledge of the object.

Step II: Notice the emptiness before the idea of the object arises.

Step III: Turn your attention around and try to find the perceiver.

Step IV: Notice there is no perceiver of the object, just perceiving, hence, no perceiver.

● ●

Principle: "Any time you become willing to experience the void, it is available." (Wilber, 1981:50)

"You cannot hear a hearer, *because there isn't one.* What you call a hearer is actually just the experience of hearing it, you don't hear hearing." "The more I try to see the seer, the more its absence begins to puzzle me.""It seems, that whenever we look for a self apart from the experience, it vanishes. The subject and object always turn out to be one." (Wilber, 1981)

Conclusion

This chapter and its exercises will bring us to a new plateau. In the next chapter, we will be asked to make another "quantum jump" and pole vault over and let go yet another idea of who we are. It is the idea of who we are that separates us from who we are. In *Star Wars: The Empire Strikes Back*, Yoda, Luke Skywalker's teacher sums it up as follows; "You must unlearn that which you have learned."

TEN

THE LAST VOYAGE

The mind is de-void of mind
H.H. Dalai Lama, San Jose, CA., 1989.

I think when Captain Kirk in "Star Trek" says, "To go where no other person has gone before," this can be seen as true in Quantum Psychology because no one will be left by the time we complete this level.

In the last chapters we have seen, and we hope experienced that all experiences, the space surrounding them, and the observer/ creator of them are one and the same. This has taken us through the following steps in our quantum journey.

As we review each quantum jump, it is important to remember two things. First of all, *Wittgenstein's ladder*. To quote world famous philosopher Ludwig Wittgenstein,

"My propositions serve as elucidations in the following way: anyone who understands me eventually recognizes them as nonsensical, when he has used them—*as steps —* to climb beyond them. (He must, so to speak, *throw away the ladder* after he has climbed up it.) (Wittgenstein, 1961:74.)

The 13th-century Sufi Poet, Rumi says it this way,

"I am a slave of whoever will not at each stage imagine that he has arrived at the end of his goal. Many a stage has to be left behind before the traveller reaches his destination." (Shah, 1976:13)

As a pole vaulter has to let go of the pole to go over to the other side, in the same way, the conclusions, beliefs, and ideas of each level are stepping stones that must be let go of to proceed on our journey.

Another metaphor is used in India called, "use a thorn to remove a thorn." Imagine a thorn stuck in your foot (the problem of not knowing who you are, separation, pain, etc.). You take another thorn (Quantum Psychology) to remove the thorn (problem of pain, etc.) that is stuck in your foot. After the thorn is removed from your foot, you throw both thorns away (the pain of separation **and** *Quantum Psychology*).

It is like the old Chinese proverb: when climbing stairs, each step is important, but to get to the next step you must go beyond or let go of the one you are standing on. Consequently, although one level might seem to contradict the one prior to it, the beginning steps are needed before we can go beyond to reach our destination. For example, in Chapter V, we discovered we are the creator of experience as well as the observer of thought, and yet in Chapter IX, we discover we are beyond the creator of our experience.

Don't be befuddled by this; you must first "get" you are the creator of your experience before you "get" that you are beyond even this concept, or as Ram Dass used to say,

"First you have to realize you are in a jail, before you can get out of it." (Dass, 1972)

Quantum Psychology Summary

Level 1: Your are the observer or witness of your experiences, i.e. thoughts, feelings, emotions and associations), therefore you are *more than* them.

Level 2: The universe is made of energy.

Level 3: The observer is the creator of the part-(icle)/mass aspect of the universe.

Level 4: The time aspect of consciousness.

Level 5: The space aspect of consciousness.

Level 6: "Everything interpenetrates everything else." (David Bohm)

Level 7: "Everything is made of emptiness and form is condensed emptiness." (Einstein) In other words, everything is made of the same substance.

Now that we have looked back at our quantum jumps, let's move forward. As mentioned in Chapter I, Henry Stapp, as quoted in F. David Peat's *Einsteins' Moon*, calls Bell's Theorem, "the most significant discovery in science."

Bell's Theorem briefly states that "reality is non-local," and there are no local causes. What does this mean? First, let us look at the first idea; no location or locality. Further on in the chapter, experiential exercises will be explored. No location means just that: there is no location. Why? A location (" I am here," "You are there,") presupposes, that there is a something that is different from something else.

"In reality everything is made of the same kind of substance, which I call *Quantum Stuff.*" (Herbert, 1985:95).

Principle: All locations can only be relative to position.

If, everything is made of the same "quantum stuff," then, there can be no position separate from any other position—hence no location.

Quantum Exercise 67

● ●

Step I: Let your eyes close, and see the empty space.

Step II: Notice that the emptiness has already organized itself into an observer observing emptiness.

Step III: Allow the emptiness to organize into the concept or part-(icle) called separate individual self.

Step IV: Allow the emptiness to organize into an idea called location, (i.e., this observing self has a different location than the observer and observed and the space which surrounds it.

Step V: Turn your attention around and "see" what, if anything, did all of that.

● ●

Here, we illustrate that there is only emptiness and condensed emptiness, and that if its all the same, even the "you" that makes that location and distinction is condensed emptiness. This begins the process of ridding ourselves of the concept of a separate local self, which *causes* a particular outcome. Why? Because everything is connected to everything else and is made of the same substance or the same Quantum Stuff.

"Suppose reality consists of ordinary objects which possess their attributes innately. Bell's Theorem requires for such a world that its objects be connected by non-local influences. Bohm's model is an example of such a world.

In this model an *invisible field* informs the electron of environmental changes with a *superluminal* response time. Bell's Theorem shows that the *faster-than-light* character of Bohm's. Without *faster-than-light* connections, an ordinary object model of realty simply cannot explain the fact. If Bell's theorem is valid, we live in a superluminal reality." (Herbert, 1985:51)

Quantum Contemplations

Contemplate that there is no location.

Contemplate a universal faster-than-light communication between people, objects, etc.

Contemplate there is no such thing as cause.

Feel, the freedom and lightness when you drop the idea of *cause*. This eliminates the tremendous pressure of, thinking if you're good, you'll get this or that, or you'll get this *because* you did that."

We use the term *local* cause, because it is impossible to reduce the universe into *this local event* here, as the cause of that event there. Everything causes everything else.

"Bell's Theorem proves the principle of local causes must be false. However, if the principle of local causes fails and, hence, the world is not the way it appears to be, then what is the true nature of the world (or the mind)? There are several mutually exclusive possibilities: the first possibility which we have discussed is that, appearance to the contrary, there really may be no such thing as separate parts in our world. In the dialect of physics, locality fails. In that case, the idea of events and autonomous happenings is an illusion. This would be the case for any separate parts that have interacted with each other at any time in the past. The possibility entails a faster-than-light communication of a type different than conventional physics can explain. In this picture, what happens here is intimately and immediately connected to what happens elsewhere in the universe, which in turn is immediately and intimately connected to what happens everywhere in the universe, and so on, simply because separate parts of the universe are not separate parts." (Zukav, 1979:296)

Location and separate parts, along with time (past, present and future), can only exist in a world where different substances exist. Since everything is made of the same substance, there can be no separate parts, no location, and no past, present, or future. Why? Because in order for location, separate parts, or past, present, and future to exist there would have to be a separate self to say it was so.

Bell's Theorem: Part 2

The second part of Bell's Theorem states that there are no local causes. The idea of no cause is also exemplified in one of Indias' most ancient and well-regarded texts; *The Yoga Vasistha.*

"a crow alights on a coconut palm tree and at that very moment a ripe coconut falls. The two *unrelated* events thus *seem* to be related in time and space, though there is no casual relationship... Such is creation. But the mind caught up in its own trap of logic questions why, *invents a why* and *a wherefore* to satisfy itself. Vasistha demands direct observation of the mind, its motion, its notions, its reasoning, the *assured* cause and the projected results, and even the *observer*, the *observed* and the *observation* —and the *realization of their indivisible unity* as infinite consciousness. (Venkatesananda, 1976).

Everything is made of the same quantum stuff, thus you could not designate something causing something else. Certainly in psychology, reducing down simple units of cause and effect seems logical. The problem is that, this implies different substances. This is imaginary, since everything is made of the same substance and *is* everything else.

Noted physicist, Dr. Feynman represents quantum stuff as a sum of possibilities.

"Everything that might have happened influences what actually does happen." (Herbert, 1985:52)

Recently, in a workshop, a participant asked me, "what about karma, the Asian concept of cause and effect? I have been to a channel, who said, so and so happened in a past life, which is why I am going through this in this life, to balance the karma." I said, "since karma can be summed up as 'what you sow, so shall you reap,' then this is true taken from a quantum perspective. If everything is made of the same quantum stuff and you *are* every-thing, and everything that happens *is* everything else, then what *you as everything* sow, so shall *you as everything* reap." This can be called Quantum Karma. Everything is everything else. Karma, as it is presently interpreted, demands the illusion of separation and the illusion of local cause A causing local effect B. This is comparable to Newton's billiard ball A causing billiard ball B to move. *Karma is what is*. From the world of a separate self, which is linear, everything appears as cause and effect, Quantum Karma is just what **is**.

In order to "experientially" understand Bell's Theorem, exer-cises are provided. Let us remember, that, with a sub-atomic lens, everything is made of the same substance, hence everything *is* the same substance. Cause and effect implies that something is separate and distinct from something else. If there are no distinctions, then there is no cause and effect. When Bell says, "no local causes," he is saying that everything is so connected to everything else, that it would be impossible to reduce the universe down into parts and conclude "this caused that."

In 1988, I had an opportunity to have lunch with noted physicist Nick Herbert, whom I've quoted many times throughout the book. At that time, I discussed with him the basic ideas of Quantum Psychology®, and, since, I'm not a physicist, I asked for *"the nod,"* i.e., telling me what I was saying was true. When I got to Bell's Theorem—no location and no local causes—Nick said, "It's the most provable thing in quantum physics."

"It wasn't until 1964 that John Bell, a physicist at the European Organization for Nuclear Research (CERN) in

Switzerland, thought of a way in which an actual experiment might be set up to settle the matter once and for all. In a brilliant mathematical proof now known as Bell's Theorem, Bell showed that if quantum theory was correct, one had to accept at least one of two options—either the world was non-objective and did not exist in a definite state, or it was 'non-local,' with instantaneous action-at-a-distance. It was as simple as that." (Talbot, 1987:32).

No local causes or no way to point to one particular thing as causing something else is the essence of this view. This leaves us without the eternal question, "Why?", because everything is made of the same substance so there can be no "Why?"—because not only does "Why?" lose its charge, but also "Where?" because there is no locally and there can be no "Where?", because location is relative to position. This also eliminates "How?" which implies separation, and "When?" since time is a concept left behind in Chapter VI.

Let us now, see if we can make this understanding more accessible through exercises. Once again, this, is a fifteen day workshop in Quantum Psychology®, and, as mentioned earlier, it would be impossible to include *everything* in the confines of these pages. We will however, present a highlighted overview to evoke possibility and openness to this quantum unity.

Let us explore this in terms of ourselves, and in the form of exercises.

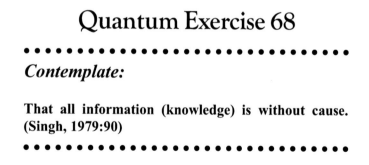

Quantum Exercise 68

• •

Contemplate:

That all information (knowledge) is without cause. (Singh, 1979:90)

• •

I'm going to use the words "knowledge" and "information" interchangeably, so that either word will mean anything you know about yourself or the world. This is suggested because in the ancient

Sanskrit text the *Siva Sutras* the sutras refer to *knowledge being bondage*, (pg. 16). Westerners confuse the word "knowledge" with the Western concept that knowledge is value. Actually, what is meant is, information you have about yourself is bondage because all information you have about yourself limits you. For example, "I am smart," or "I am ugly," or "I am stupid," are all information you have about yourself. Therefore, all information defines and limits your experience of yourself. As discussed in Chapter III, you are beyond this constricted definition.

• •

This format may be used by the rotating group facilitator.

Let your eyes close and move into a quiet space. As any information about yourself comes into your awareness, contemplate the possibility that all information is without cause. Contemplate any information as being without any cause. Whenever you're ready, bring your awareness back to the room, notice where you're sitting, and let your eyes open.

• •

One student told me, "It's sort of a sticky issue for me, because I think I've never felt that anything came from cause or that I see things connect the way most people see them. It has sometimes made me feel as if I were crazy. To think that the way we function is from cause and effect could be a grounding mechanism, but I've never had that to ground myself with. It's never meant anything to me. I'm scared that if nothing connects then my whole perception of reality gets screwed, and then I feel really weird."

Another student reported, "My experience was that there was just no power in my thoughts or ideas or knowledge, just nothing connected to them." I replied, "Most people give their power away to thoughts, people, events or situations. By taking your power back from people you feel more power—this is empowerment."

In other words, if you have been in a relationship in which how you felt about yourself was dependent upon how the other person felt about you at that moment, they had the power. Your okayness was dependent upon them. In the same way, if you have a thought called, "I want to go to Hawaii on a vacation" and give your power to that, then that thought will have power over you. The next thing you know you're working overtime to pay for your trip to Hawaii: Who has the power? The thought of a trip to Hawaii has the power, because you're reacting to it; but you can pull your energy from it, and it will then have no power over you. You can *choose* to do it, or *choose* to not do it.

Here is an interesting issue brought up by a physicist in my workshop: "I couldn't help but translate, 'This thought has no cause,' into 'This thought has no source.' Then I said that I generate not only thought but, as a scientist, I generate facts. To say that they don't have a source is to say that I don't exist. I couldn't deal with it." I suggested to him that he had fused together his own existence with facts and thoughts.

Quantum Exercises (Reviewed)

Quantum Exercise 69

• •

The world as empty space and part-(icles).

For a minute or two, look at your hand. Pull your attention backward into the emptiness prior to the information or idea of your hand. Without blinking, imagine that your hand is made of tiny particles floating in empty-space. Now allow your body to be experienced as part-(icles) floating in empty space. Look around the room at different objects; de-focus your eyes allowing yourself to see objects, the wall, a couch, etc. as made of part-(icles) floating in empty space. Notice how this experience is freeing and expansive. This simple exercise can be practiced anywhere.

Einstein explains (as does the Buddhist *Heart Sutra*) that these part-(icles) are made of condensed emptiness,

and that the emptiness is made of thinned out and liquefied particles. As you do the exercise, contemplate, "Who is doing this process?"

• •

Quantum Contemplation

Contemplate that I am condensed emptiness. Experience yourself as condensed emptiness.

Quantum Exercise 70

• •

Step I: See the emptiness in front of you.

Step II: Take some emptiness and condense it into anything solid, e.g., thought, feeling, etc..

Step III: Thin it out into emptiness.

Step IV: Do this several times (condensing and thinning).

Step V: Experience the "you" that is doing all this as condensed emptiness.

• •

Nothing Does Nothing to Nothing

This probably is the most interesting part. The one who is doing these exercises is made of the same condensed emptiness as the thought, feeling, chair, or table.

Quantum Exercise 71

• •

Location

Do this guided by a group facilitator.

Step I: Notice the emptiness in front of you.

Step II: Allow the emptiness to condense and become an experience.

Step III: Allow the emptiness to be an observer of the experience.

Step IV: Allow the observer (emptiness) to create the concept of location.

Step V: Pretend the concept is true.

Step VI: Pretend you are not pretending it is true.

Step VII: See the observer, the experience, the concept of location, and the concept of cause and effect as the same substance, emptiness and condensed emptiness.

Step VIII: Turn your attention around and see if you can find the one who did all of that.

• •

Quantum Exercise 72

• •

Cause and effect.

A group facilitator guides the group as follows:

Step I: Notice the emptiness in front of you.

Step II: Allow the emptiness to condense and be- come an experience.

Step III: Allow and designate part of the emptiness as an observer of the experience.

Step IV   Condense emptiness down creating the con- cept of location.

Step V: Condense emptiness down creating the con- cept of cause and effect.

Step VI: Pretend these concepts are true.

Step VII: Pretend you are not pretending these con- cepts are true.

Step VIII: See the observer, the experience, the con- cept of location, and the concept of cause and effect as the same substance, emptiness and condensed emptiness.

Step IX: Turn your attention around and see if you can find the one who did all of that.

• •

Even the observer or witness is made of condensed emptiness, which means that not only is everything the same, but the "you", you thought you were, is made of the same condensed emptiness as the chair you are sitting on. This means that the chair you are sitting on exists only as long as the condensed emptiness you call "you" exists to see it.

"There is no reality in the absence of observation." (Herbert, 1985:17)

Quantum Contemplation

Contemplate for a moment that the observer the observed and the contemplator are all made of condensed emptiness.

Actually the whole phenomenological universe and you are made of condensed emptiness, i.e. the same "quantum stuff." You only exist as the seer apart from the seen as an apparent condensed emptiness, *pretending* you are not a condensed emptiness. Therefore, you the observer and the experience are all the same condensed emptiness. Stated another way, experiences only exist as long as you don't know who you are. Once you know you and the experience are made of the same condensed emptiness—there is no longer an experience. Once you know who you are, there is no experiencer or experience, there is just emptiness, or a no-experience experience of the quantum field.

In the Hindu scripture *The Ramayana*, Lord Ram, who is quantum consciousness, is served by Hanuman. One of Hanuman's clearest statements to Lord Ram is, "when I don't know who I am, I serve you. When I know who I am, I am you."

This, in essence, is Hanuman, He serves quantum when he perceives separation. When He is quantum or Ram then he knows himself, and is quantum (Ram). Hanuman actually never changes: Hanuman is Ram, Ram is Hanuman. In the same way, we are in quantum consciousness and *are* quantum consciousness even if we don't know it.

In the quantum understanding, nothing does nothing to nothing, and *even this is not true*, because it would only be true if someone observed it. *Therefore Quantum Consciousness IS, and Quantum Consciousness isn't.* It is like the old joke, "How many Zen Masters does it take to change a light bulb?" "Two. One to do it, and one not to do it."

Quantum Exercise 73

● ●

This exercise is an extension illustrating turning your attention around. It comes from Douglas Harding's book, *On Having No Head*. (Harding, 1986:42)*

Step I: Take your index finger and point it toward your head.

Step II: Notice if there is anything there.

● ●

This was the experience I had when I was sitting in meditation in 1988, when I decided to look for the one who was meditating. There was no one there.

Quantum Exercise 74

● ●

From Douglas Harding.

To be done in a group, with the rotating facilitator reading the following.

Let your eyes close and ask yourself:

1. Going on your present experience without using your memory or mind, "are you a man , a woman, or neither?"

---

*"To turn around the arrow of ones attention ... if only he is willing to drop for a moment opinions about himself based on hearsay and memory and imagination, and to rely on PRESENT EVIDENCE."

2. Going on your present experience without using your memory or mind, "are you in a body, out of a body, or neither?"

3. Going on your present experience without using your memory or mind, "are you form, formless, or neither?"

4.Going on your present experience without using your memory or mind, "are you defined, undefined, or neither?"

● ●

Often times in workshops, and with many clients I've seen, the response is the same, "Neither." This demonstrates that people are experiencing themselves beyond "normal" and "conventional" definitions.

"This way .. Seeing into Nothingness - is the very start of a Spiritual Life."(Harding, 1988)

Quantum Exercise 75

● ●

With eyes closed and attention turned around, the group leader says:

1. **On present evidence without using your memory or mind, "is there anything you could do to be more perfect?"**

2. **On present evidence without using your memory or mind, "do you have qualities?"**

3. **On present evidence without using your memory or mind, "is there anyway to make you better?"**

4. **On present evidence without using your memory or mind, "has this always been there?"**

5. On present evidence without using your memory or mind, "would this be affected if you remembered it or not?"

6. On present evidence without using your memory or mind, "is there anything you could add to this to make yourself better, purer, healed, or closer to God?"

7. On present evidence without using your memory or mind, "does this need to be reframed, healed or changed in any way?"

The Quantum Consciousness Process

The Quantum Consciousness process is the highlight of this approach. These two processes, when understood and experienced, leave the practitioner in the no-state state of the non-being being. Therefore, not only is nothing occurring; there is neither being nor a non-being. Try it and notice what occurs.

● ●

Part I

To be done with a rotating facilitator reading the following:

Step I: Close your eyes and notice that you are the background of your experience.

Step II: Allow the emptiness to condense into form and become an experience.

Step III: Pretend you don't know the form is condensed emptiness.

Step IV: Be aware that the form is condensed back-
            ground or emptiness.

Step V: Turn your attention around and see if you
            can find what, if anything, is doing this.

● ●

Part II

*This format is suggested for use by a rotating group
facilitator.*

(eyes closed.)

Step I: Be the background of your experience.

Step II: Allow the background to be emptiness and
            the foreground, you're looking into, to be
            thinned-out emptiness.

Step III: Pretend you don't know the background is
            emptiness, and the emptiness in the fore-
            ground is thinned-out form.

Step IV: Allow the emptiness of the background and
            the emptiness of the foreground and you to
            all be seen as emptiness.

Step V: Turn your attention around and notice what,
            if anything, is doing all of this.

Part III

To be read out loud by rotating group facilitator.

Step I: Experience yourself as the background of an experience and the experience as foreground.

Step II: Notice the observer of the experience.

Step III: Notice that you are the background of the observer.

Step IV: Notice that the observer and the experience it observes is foreground.

Step V: Condense the background making it into the experience in the foreground.

Step VI: Thin-out the observer making it background.

Step VII: Make the experience the background.

Step VIII: Make any you that is being experienced in the foreground into the background by thinning it out.

Step IX: By turning your attention around, notice there is no "you" doing this exercise!

Here we see the final level of Quantum Psychology®, *Quantum Consciousness*. *Modern psychology is interested in the foreground, Quantum Psychology is interested in the background, and the understanding that foreground is background and background is foreground. More importantly, background, foreground, and the observer of both are one and the same, which means no background or foreground. And, as for the "you" you call yourself, well whether it be perceived as background or foreground, it doesn't matter since they are the same. This means that the concept of a self or no-self does not leave us with an absence, rather it leaves us with a presence of pure isness.*

> "No one has influenced more of our notions of what the Quantum world is more than Danish physicist Neils Bohr, and it is Bohr who put forth one of Quantum Physics most outrageous claims: there is *no deep reality*. Far from being a crank or minority position, 'There is no deep reality' represents the prevailing doctrine of established physics." (Herbert, 1985:16)

This means everything *is* the same substance—hence, there is no deep reality nor is there not deep reality—everything just *is*.

Quantum consciousness is not quantum consciousness at all; it could only be called so if someone were there to perceive it.

So now with no quantum consciousness in the absence of an observer, what are we left with? With ourselves, or as David Bohm calls it, "unbroken wholeness." Bohm insists, "There is no quantum world." So too, Quantum Psychology suggests that with pure isness there is no "where" to be left, no one to be left, nowhere to go.

From pure isness, Bell's Theorem of no local causes and, in essence, no location, never arises, because there is no separate self to bring up the concept of "this causing that" or "this being separate from that"—*therefore, there is no such thing as distance* from one object or person to another.

Quantum Exercise 76

● ●

"If one perceives the cosmos as mere jugglery conjured up by some juggler or magician, or sees the world as a painting...then they will experience great happiness." (Singh, 1979:92)

Practice

The following format may be used by the rotating group facilitator.

Close your eyes for a few minutes and think about or imagine that the world is just like juggling, like something produced by a juggler in the circus, and that everything is being constantly juggled very spontaneously, almost like a magician's trick and that, somehow, everyone and everything landed this way. Let your mind expand to imagine that the world is like juggling, a magician's trick. Somehow, it all landed here, and everybody somehow lands where they do.

Contemplate the freedom, if the world is just a magician's trick.

Now open your eyes and look around the room and see if you can imagine that everything has been juggled somehow like a magician's trick, and lands where it does *randomly*.

• •

Quantum Contemplations

Contemplate there is no one who is in charge of the universe.

Contemplate the emptiness is in charge.

With no separate individual self to perceive it, there could not be a cause, an effect, a locality, or something or someone in charge of what happens. Here, Bohm's unbroken wholeness is experienced: no causes and since no causes, no effects. Stated another way; *The cause is the effect.*

World famous philosopher and political activist Mahatma Gandhi understood this. Gandhi's policy of non-violence was used by Martin Luther King in the 1960s. Mahatma Gandhi emphasized that people felt that the *end* justifies the *means*. Gandhi understood that *the means and the end were the same.* This is why he used passive resistance and non-violence to get the English to leave India in the 1940s.

There never has been nor will there be an individual experience of quantum consciousness or enlightenment. Since that could only exist if there were a *separate* you to declare that it existed. No you— no *individual* enlightenment.

"There is no Quantum World," warned Bohr, "there is only an *abstract quantum description.*" (Herbert, 1985:22)

Eleven

Consciousness

This is the end, beautiful friend, the end. This is the end, my only friend, the end...picture what will be so limitless and free...

Jim Morrison

For thousands of years, people have been attempting to discern the nature of consciousness. As we bring this book to a close, it seems appropriate to look at consciousness in general, and specifically how it applies to Quantum Psychology.

Consciousness has been defined as an ability to know distinctions. Self-consciousness is consciousness of oneself or the imaginary distinction between subject (observer) and knowing object (self).

Consciousness, from the perspective of Quantum Psychology, can be defined in two ways. First, consciousness is that which discerns distinctions. For example, you might say, "I am conscious that you like television and I like reading." Here we have the consciousness to notice the difference between *me* liking television and *you* liking reading. Secondly, I am conscious that reading is different from television. In both cases there is consciousness of contrasts or distinctions, i.e, the you reading being different from the you watching television. As mentioned in chapter IX and X, without *contrasts* there could be no experience. Consciousness is creative because consciousness is that which lets us know of contrasts, distinctions, and Bohm's explicate order. What consciousness does not let us know is Bohm's implicate order (the underlying unity). Why? Because where consciousness is, the unity cannot be seen; the function of consciousness is to see contrasts and differences.

A student came to Nisargadatta Maharaj and said, "I want to be happy." Maharaj replied, "That's nonsense; happiness is where the "I" isn't." He was saying that happiness exists at the implicate level where there is no consciousness just emptiness which knows no distinctions or a separate "I" separation.

Consciousness is where the "I" *is*, and consciousness is where the distinctions of the explicate order take place. Consciousness does not exist at an implicate level, because at an implicate level there are no distinctions or contrasts, just pure *Isness*. This means that what you call an individual self or "you" can never know the underlying unity, because the underlying unity doesn't have *consciousness* of a "you" separate from something to be known or to know about. *What is consciousness?* **Condensed emptiness.** Therefore, to know consciousness as condensed emptiness and emptiness as thinned-out consciousness is to know the non-dual (implicate), dual (explicate) nature of the universe. Simply put, ultimately, *the implicate is the explicate, the explicate is the implicate.*

A French psychiatrist came to Nisargadatta Maharaj and began a long-winded question about past lives, future lives, karma, credits and debits, etc. I don't remember this gentleman's question completely, but I do remember Maharaj's answer. "Who told you that you exist?" Maharaj asked. The French psychiatrist looked at his wife; his wife looked at him but remained silent. Maharaj said, "Consciousness told you you exist, if you understand just this, it's enough."

Once again, he was re-stating the definition of consciousness as that which knows distinctions or the explicate order. Consciousness is the observer and observed, knower and known, experiencer and experience. Without consciousness to know distinctions, there would just be the implicate order of quantum *Isness*. Therefore, consciousness tells you you exist as a separate self. The concept of existence or non-existence does not arise or exist in emptiness— only in consciousness. It can then be said, consciousness is condensed emptiness, and emptiness is undifferentiated consciousness; (i.e., consciousness without distinctions).

Quantum Contemplation

Could there be an experience if there were no conscious- ness or that which knows the experience?

Quantum Exercise 77

• •

Step I: Let your eyes close, and see the emptiness in front of you.

Step II: Allow the emptiness to condense and organ- ize itself into the concept of consciousness by adding the idea of distinctions and con- trasts. Allow the empty space to condense and organize itself into the concept called "creating".

Step III: Allow this newly formed idea of conscious- ness to do and create what it creates.

• •

Often in workshops, people feel as though they were left with nothing or emptiness. This quantum jump allows us to view the nothing and the something as the same.

Quantum Contemplation

Contemplate the emptiness is thinned-out something, and the something is condensed emptiness.

The Emptiness is Alive

The good news from this understanding is that it leaves us with *total possibility*, since we (condensed emptiness) can actually never know what will come or go or, more simply, what emptiness will condense into and appear and what form or experiences will thin-out and disappear. The bad news is that for some of us who like order and control this can be disconcerting. As was mentioned briefly in Chapter II, it is the resistance to randomness, chaos, etc. that causes so many of our problems. Stated another way, systems and models of consciousness are created as a way of *resisting* randomness.* Even Albert Einstein, a major architect of quantum mechanics, and a Nobel Prize winner, went to his grave unable to accept what he had proven. Einstein's "God does not throw dice with the universe," underscores his inability to accept "randomness" and *his* resistance to chaos.

We must appreciate that consciousness which is condensed emptiness is emptiness. More importantly, emptiness cannot know itself. *Consciousness, therefore, is the way emptiness knows itself.*

"Consciousness creates Reality." (Herbert, 1985:24)

Eugene Wignor, noted physicist, says,

"It is not possible to formulate the laws of quantum mechanics in a fully consistent way without reference to consciousness... It will remain remarkable in whatever way our future concepts develop, that the very study of the external world led to the conclusion that the content of consciousness is the ultimate Reality." (Herbert, 1985:25-26)

Re-stated, consciousness is the way you can formulate a self which can say there is an ultimate reality. If there is no consciousness and just emptiness there is no ultimate reality because there is no separate individual to say there is an ultimate reality.

Here is testimony to what I have called the "quantum force." A force or idea contained within emptiness, made of emptiness itself

---

*This will be the total topic of my forthcoming book *The Tao of Chaos: Quantum Consciousness Volume II.* The book deals with the new science of Chaos and its relationship to psychology.

is the vehicle or medium of emptiness, to know itself: consciousness. It is this quantum force or consciousness (which is made of emptiness) which constructs and de-constructs thoughts, feelings, emotions, and even the "I" we call ourselves in a random way.

Principle: Consciousness is condensed emptiness and is the creative vehicle of emptiness. In quantum terms, the quantum force, which is a condensation of the quantum field, is the creative vehicle of the quantum field.

An observer who observes differences and distinctions, is still consciousness observing consciousness or consciousness observing itself.

Principle: Since consciousness is condensed emptiness and is the creative aspect of emptiness, then consciousness *is* emptiness. Therefore, consciousness can never lose or find itself.

Quantum Contemplations

Contemplate the you who observes is made of consciousness.

Contemplate the object (thought, feeling, etc.) is made of consciousness.

Contemplate the subject observer is made of the same consciousness as its object (thought or feeling).

Contemplate you are consciousness whether you are aware of it or not. This is quantum consciousness.

Contemplate that bondage is just a thought construct, or an idea, or a belief or condensed emptiness. (Singh, 1979:24)

Contemplate freedom is just a concept or condensed emptiness. (Singh, 1979:24)

Quantum Exercise 78

• •

To be read out loud by a rotating group facilitator.

(eyes closed)

Step I: See the emptiness in front of you.

Step II: Allow the emptiness to condense slightly and create the idea of consciousness.

Step III: Allow the newly formed concept of consciousness to create the idea of losing itself and finding itself.

Step IV: Pretend you are that consciousness trying to be found.

Step V: Pretend you're not pretending to be the lost consciousness trying to be found.

Step VI: Pretend you are the lost consciousness which is found and enlightened.

Step VII: Turn your attention around and notice the emptiness that has done all of that.

Step VIII: Contemplate "I AM THAT undifferentiated consciousness."

• •

The beauty of developing this quantum awareness is, that everything is seen as the *same* rather than *different* than everything else. Modern psychology, has developed a system focusing on individual differences, whereas, Quantum Psychology offers a view of the world as a whole, unified, connected field.

How can this aid us in our journey through life? Let's explore several other quantum exercises and see how using them can help us feel more connected and alive.

Quantum Exercise 79

• •

Information not only appears in me, but all objects have information. (Singh, 1979:94-95)

Practice

Group facilitator:

Feeling your body supported and noticing your breathing, go into a quiet space. I would like you now to consider for a minute whatever information you have about yourself. For example, you're a woman, you're a man, you're tall, you're short, fat or thin, or some other piece of information. Take a moment to observe that information. Now contemplate that not only do I have information about myself, but all objects—pictures, couches, chairs, lamps—everything has information inside itself. Now, letting your eyes open, I'd like you to look around the room imagining that everything— couches and chairs, everything—has information about itself. You might want to imagine what that information is.

• •

One student commented, "I felt less alone and more connected by the possibility that everything has information about itself, things seem more alive."

Quantum Exercise 80

• •

Desires do not only appear inside me, but they also appear inside other objects. (Singh, 1979)

The exercise begins with eyes closed for two or three minutes and then finishes with two or three minutes with eyes open.

Practice

Group facilitator:

Feeling your body being physically supported, watch your breathing. Observing, notice a cavalcade or a parade of your desires. Watch, then, from a distance, as if you were in a movie theater watching the desires going by on the screen. Take a few minutes to do that.

Consider for another minute that the desires don't only appear inside of me, but that all objects—chairs, couches, pictures, lamps, everything—have desires. Just for a moment, expand, and imagine everything having desires.

Very gently, let your eyes open. And imagine all the objects in the room and people as having desires. Guess what those desires are. Continue to look at the different objects and imagine what their deepest desire is. See if you can keep that awareness for a few minutes.

• •

"When I did this exercise one student shared, "I eventually got to a chair just wanting to be a chair and a couch just wanting to be a couch. And the fantasy I imagined was that a couch wants to be a chair, and the chair wants to be a different color!"

One person experienced, "I got the basic impression that everything desired just to be. It was very freeing to realize that, because it was as if everybody and everything just wants to exist. Then I thought, Why are we always doing this stuff about things not existing, and that whole side of Indian, or whatever, philosophy?" I decided it was better to concentrate on the being, or the is-ness, or whatever. And that was very nice."

I replied, "It's very difficult to be in the world and practice (not this, not this) Vedanta. It's much easier to practice Kashmir Shavism or Tantric Yoga (and this, and this). That's the primary reason that yogis have a hard time implanting themselves in America. It's very difficult to say to Westerners "not this, not this." Baba Muktananda was a pure Vedantan until he came to America. He was very practical, and that's when he adopted Kashmir Shavism. Instead of "not this, not this, not this," he adopted "and this, and this, and this," which is very appropriate to Western culture, because you can't say to your landlord, "not this, not this," even if you want too.

So, as we begin to appreciate the creative aspect of consciousness which makes us aware of our distinctions, we can appreciate, that consciousness must be there, otherwise, there could be no self to know itself.

Let us now look at the physical body as consciousness.

Quantum Exercise 81

• •

The body is consciousness (Singh, 1979:97)

(eyes closed)

Step I: Experience your body as made of consciousness.

Step II: Experience the possibility that every person is made of consciousness.

Step III: Experience the possibility that all objects are made of consciousness.

Practice

Rotating group facilitator:

(eyes closed)

Now we're going to be working on seeing our body as consciousness. We will sit for about fifteen minutes and then another few minutes with eyes open. Find a quiet space inside yourself. In this exercise, experience that your body is made of consciousness. The way to do that is to allow your body to be made of consciousness in one spontaneous "movement" rather than doing it piece by piece. Hold the feeling, maybe even the sound of the body as consciousness.

What does your body look like? What is it feeling? What sounds do you hear when your whole body is consciousness? Continue experiencing your body in one "movement," being made of consciousness. If any thoughts, feelings or sensations come-up, see them as made of consciousness. Experience your skin boundary as made of consciousness.

Now allow and consider that the same consciousness that is in your body is in other bodies and that all bodies are made of the same consciousness. Now experience that all objects or things in the world are made of consciousness appearing in different shapes or forms. Lastly, experience the doer of this exercise as being made of the same consciousness as everything else. Very gently, let your eyes open, making eye contact with other people in the room, experiencing that their bodies and your body are made of the same consciousness. Continue to make eye contact with other people in the room with that awareness.

● ●

One workshop participant said, "I felt like my body was in *Star Trek* where they are beaming people up and their body shimmers in that in-between place between being solid and disappearing. My body shimmered."

Let us take this one step further.

Quantum Exercise 82

● ●

Focus on the universe as your body. (Singh, 1979:62)

Practice

Rotating group facilitator:

(eyes closed)

Focus on your physical body. Very gently begin to experience that everything in the room is your physical body, every person, everything. Just expand so that everything in the room is part of your physical body. Stretch your awareness to include everything in the room.

Then, very gently include the apartment complex or house that you live in. Let your awareness stretch, expand, to include your apartment complex. Then expand to include your neighborhood. Include all that in your awareness. Notice that at first there might be a little resistance, but just expand gently to include the entire neighborhood in your awareness. Gently expand to include all of your city so that it's all inside your awareness. Gently include your city and the surrounding ones in your awareness. Let your awareness spread to include the whole state. Let your awareness expand to include neighboring states. Let you awareness expand until your awareness includes your part of the country, then your half of the country, east or west of

the Mississippi. Expand to include all of that inside your awareness. Now include the entire United States inside your awareness. Just gently expand to include it. Then drift into Canada, and then into Central America, South America. It's easier and easier to include the oceans on both sides, Atlantic and Pacific. Include Asia and India and Southeast Asia. It becomes much easier to include it. Africa. Europe. Keep expanding so you include the whole planet inside your awareness. Continue to include the solar system, the galaxy, and the universe inside your awareness. Whenever you are ready, bring your attention back to the room. Let your eyes open.

● ●

How can this be of value? All part-(icles) or universes, whether individual or collective, are made of the same consciousness (condensed emptiness) as all others. As in parallel universe theory, all are part-(icles) in emptiness, as mentioned in Chapters IX and X. They are the same. This means that, metaphorically speaking, we all have the same mother and father—*emptiness* and *condensed emptiness*. This understanding is valuable, because wars, interpersonal conflicts, and intrapersonal conflicts can be reconciled through the understanding that we are all made of the same substance and are the same substance.

In the Buddhist system, it is said that we have all incarnated so many times that everyone has been your mother, and you have been everyone else's mother. This metaphor translates as, "We are all made of the same substance and therefore are one, whether we are aware of it or not;" therefore everyone, subatomically is every one else's mother and father because they are all made of the same Quantum stuff. Jokingly, in a workshop I said, "This could be a horrifying thought for many of us who come from abusive homes, but think of the economic possibilities for those of us who are therapists—an eternal client!"

Since so many groups, wars, and conflicts are created through the use of symbols, as a way of creating differences and separations, let us now take a look to see how this understanding can help to alleviate these internal/external controversies.

A symbol can be defined as,

"Something used or regarded as standing for or representing something else." (American College Dictionary).

Symbols carry condensed feelings of compacted consciousness. Often, a symbol can be powerful, because of meanings that have been placed upon it, while the emptiness it emerged from, as well as what it is made of, goes unnoticed.

Quantum Exercise 83

• •

Find the empty space before the emergence of any religious symbols.

The purpose of this exercise is to notice the empty space prior to a religious or spiritual symbol, such as a cross, Jewish star, mandala, statue, crystal, etc. I am going to ask you to notice a symbol. It doesn't matter what it is. You'll be surprised how many good or bad feelings (energy) you have attached to it. I want you then to go back into the empty space from which the symbol arose, to the empty space prior to the symbol.

Practice

Format for use by the rotating group facilitator:

With eyes closed take a deep breath. I'd like you to develop an image, or let an image come to you, of a spiritual, religious, or political symbol. Notice what positive or negative feelings you have about the symbol. Then expand your awareness and find the emptiness prior to the emergence of that symbol. Let another symbol come up into your awareness. Notice the image, good or bad, and find the empty space that symbol came from. Now let another symbol come up to your awareness. Notice the energy, and find the empty space that symbol came from. Allow another symbol to come into your awareness, and again, locate the empty space that symbol came from. And finally, one more symbol. Notice the energy attached to it, and find the empty space. Notice that the symbol is made of condensed emptiness, and that all symbols are made of the same substance. This time stay in the empty space. Go deeply into the void prior to the emergence of any or all symbols. Stay there. Whenever you're ready to begin coming back, bring your awareness back here to the room, and allow your eyes to open.

• •

A student commented, "That was really refreshing. It was kind of like going into outer space. I saw all of these symbols spilling around, and I would create a feeling about one and throw it back, and there was always that space."

Quantum Exercise 84
• •

(eyes closed)

Step I: Notice the emptiness in front of you.

Step II: Allow the emptiness in front of you to organize itself into consciousness of a symbol (a flag, a religious symbol, etc.)

Step III: Merge with and experience the consciousness of the symbol.

Step IV: Step back and notice the empty space that surrounds the consciousness of the symbol.

Step V: See the consciousness of the symbol as condensed emptiness.

Step VI: See the consciousness you call "you" as the same condensed emptiness as the consciousness of the symbol.

•••••••••••••••••••••••••••••••••••

With this understanding, where is there to go? Here, once again, we are asked to acknowledge the unity of everything, a major leap, yet one that, from the point of view of consciousness (distinctions), *seems* important.

Is Emptiness Something to be Afraid of?

Often in workshops, people will say, "Well this leaves me with nothing." On the contrary, it leaves you with everything. Noted physicist J. A. Wheeler says, "Nothingness is the building block of the universe." The nothing is alive! Nothing is in charge.

Quantum Exercise 85

•••••••••••••••••••••••••••••••

(eyes closed)

Step I: See the emptiness in front of you.

Step II: Notice how the emptiness becomes something (thought, feeling, image, etc.)

Step III: Notice that you are made of the same emptiness that has organized itself into a you, or a separate self.

•••••••••••••••••••••••••••••••

Quantum Contemplations

Contemplate the nothing becomes thoughts, feelings, images, chairs, etc.

Contemplate the nothing becomes this "you," and the nothing becomes this "not you."

Contemplate everything (experiences, actions, the movement of the eyes, smells, understanding) is made of that emptiness and occurs or doesn't occur through or by emptiness.

Where Does this Leave us?

Developing a quantum context does not exclude anything; rather, it includes modern psychology, Eastern or Middle Eastern philosophy and practices. What Quantum Psychology is pointing to is a direction, or a way of viewing the problem of human suffering.

This book is not an end but rather a *beginning*, a place where we can all join hands and develop our own approaches to re-membering and re-connecting to that underlying quantum unity. *The quantum approach does not exclude anything. It includes everything and everyone.* This book is a call to ourselves as brothers and sisters, to connect at this invisible quantum level.

A very famous Hindu Teacher, Ramana Maharishi was on his deathbed, when one of his disciples said, "Please don't go." He replied, "Where can I go?" He was saying, it's all the same quantum stuff. Where is there that is different from here?

Ultimately, however, quantum consciousness does not exist. Why? Because there would have to be something separate from it to say it did. So, quantum consciousness leaves us here, and so do I.

EPILOGUE

What would a Quantum World be like.

Imagine:

John Lennon

Imagine there's no Heaven
It's easy if you try
No Hell below us
Above us only sky
Imagine all the people
Living for Today

Imagine there's no countries
It isn't hard to do
Nothing to kill or die for
And no religion too.
Imagine all the people
Living life in peace.

You may say I'm a dreamer
But I'm not the only one
I hope someday you'll join us
And the world will be as *one*.

Imagine no possessions,
I wonder if you can
No need for greed or hunger
A brotherhood/sisterhood of man
Imagine all the people
Sharing all the world

You may say I'm a dreamer
But I'm not the only one
I hope one day you'll join us,
And the world will be as *ONE*.

BIBLIOGRAPHY

Almaas, A.H. *The Void*. York Beach, ME: Samuel Weiser, Inc., 1986.

American College Dictionary. New York: Random House, 1963.

Bahirgit, B. P. *The Amritanubhava of Jnanadeva*. Bombay: Sirur Press, 1963.

Bentov, Itzhak. *Stalking the Wild Pendulum: On the Mechanics of Consciousness*. Rochester, VT: Destiny Books, 1977.

Berne, Eric. *Games People Play*. New York: Grove Press, 1964.

Besant, Ann and Leadbeater, C.W. *Thought Forms*. Wheaton IL: The Theosophical Publishing House, 1969.

Blank, Gertrude R. and Rubin. *Ego Psychology II*. New York: Columbia University Press, 1974

Bohm, David. *The Enfolding-Unfolding Universe: a Conversation with David Bohm*.

_____. *Quantum Theory*. London: Constable, 1951.

_____. *Wholeness and the Implicate Order*. London: Ark Paperbacks, 1980.

_____ and Peat, David F. *Science, Order and Creativity*. New York: Bantam Books, 1987.

_____. *Unfolding Meaning*. London: Ark Paperbacks, 1985.

Boslough, John. *Stephen Hawking's Universe*. New York: Avon Books, 1985.

Briggs, John and Peat, David F. *Looking Glass Universe: The Emerging Science of Wholeness.* New York: Simon & Schuster, 1984.

Capek, M. *The Philisophical Impact of Contemporary Pysics.* Princton, NJ: D. Van Nostrand, 1961.

Capra, Fritjof. *The Tao of Physics.* New York: Bantam Books, 1976.

Cayce, Edgar. *Edgar Cayce on ESP.* New York: Paperback Library, 1967.

Dass, Ram. *The Only Dance There Is.* New York: Bantam, 1972

Davies, Paul and Gribbin, John. *The Myth of Matter: Dramatic Discoveries That Challenge Our Understanding of Physical Reality.* New York: Touchstone Books, Simon and Schuster, 1992.

Davis, Martha, Fannie, Patrick and McKay, Mathew. *Thoughts and Feelings: The Art of Cognitive Stress Intervention.* Richmond, CA: New Harbinger Publications, 1981.

DeWitt, C. and Wheeler, J.A. *Battelle Renconties,* "Superspace and the Nature of Quantum Geometrodynamics: 1967 Lectures in Mathematics and Physics". New York: W.A. Benjamin, 1968.

Erickson, M. H. and Rossi, E.L. *Hypnotherapy: An Exploratory Casebook.* New York: Irvington, 1979.

_____ and Rossi, E.L. *The February Man: Facilitating New Identity in Hypnotherapy.*

Fung, Yu-lan. *A Short History of Chinese Philosophy.* New York: Macmillan, 1958.

Godman, David. *Be As You Are: The Teachings of Ramana Maharshi.* Arkana, London, 1985.

Goldstein, Joseph. *The Experience of Insight.* Boston/London: Shambhala,1987.

_____ and Kornfield, Jack. *Seeking the Heart of Wisdom: The Path of Insight Meditation.* Boston/London: Shambhala, 1987.

Govinda, L. A., *Foundations of Tibetan Mysticism,* New York: Samuel Weiser, 1974.

Haley, J. *Advanced Techniques of Hypnosis and Therapy: Selected Papers of Milton H. Erickson, M.D.* New York: Grune & Stratton, 1967.

Harding, D. E. *On Having No Head: Zen and the Rediscovery of the Obvious.* London: Arkana (Routledge & Kegan Paul), 1986.

_____. *The Little Book of Life and Death.* London: Arkana, 1988.

Hawking, Stephen. *A Brief History of Time.* New York: Bantam Publishing Co., 1988.

Herbert, Nick. *Quantum Reality: Beyond the New Physics.* New York: Anchor Press, 1985.

Hoffer, Eric. *The True Believer.* New York: Harper and Row, 1951.

Hoffman, Yoel. *The Sound of the One Hand.* New York: Basic Books, 1975.

Hua, Master Tripitaka. *Shurangama Sutra.* San Francisco, CA: Buddhist Text Translation Society, 1977.

_____. *The Heart Sutra and Commentary.* San Francisco, CA: Buddhist Text Translation Society, 1980.

Isherwood, Christopher and Prabhavanda, Swami. *How to Know God: the Yoga Aphorisms of Patanjali.* California: New American Library, 1953.

Jagadiswarananda, Swami. *Devi Mahatmyam Sri Ramakrishna Math.* Madras, 1978.

Jung, Carl, *The Structure and Dynamics of the Psyche, Vol. III,* The Collected Works of Carl Jung, Translated by R.F.C. Hall, Bolingen Series XX, Princeton, NJ: Princeton University Press, 1960.

Khanna Madhu. *Yantra The Tantric Symbol of Cosmic Unity.* London: Thames and Hudson Ltd., 1979.

Korzybski, Alfred. *Science and Sanity: An Introduction to Non-Aristotelian Systems and General Semantics.* Lancaster, PA: International Non-Aristotelian Library Publishing Company, 1933.

Lopez, Donald. *The Heart Sutra Explained.* New York: State University of New York Press, 1988.

Maharshi, Ramana. *Gems from Bhagavan Sri Ramanashram.* Tiruvannamali, 1965.

_____. *The Spiritual Teaching of Ramana Maharshi.* Boulder/ London: Shambhala, 1972.

_____. *Talks with Sri Ramana Maharshi Ramanashram.* S. India, 1978.

Masters, Robert and Houston, Jean. *Mind Games: The Guide to Inner Space.* New York: Dell Publishing Company, 1972.

Mookerjit, Ajit. *Tantra Asana. A Way to Self-Realization.* Basel, Paris, New Delhi: Ravi Kumar, 1971.

_____. *Tantra Art—Its Philosophy and Physics.* Basil, Paris, New Delhi: Ravi Kumar, 1971.

Morrison, Philip and Phylis. *Powers of Ten.* New York: Scientific American Library, 1982.

Mudallar Devaraja. *Day by Day with Bhajavan.* Tiruvannameli, S. India: Sri Rananashram, 1977.

Muktananda, Swami. *I Am That: The Science of Hamsa.* New York: S.Y.D.A. Foundation, 1978.

_____. *Play of Consciousness.* Ganeshpuri: Shree Gurudev Ashram, 1974.

Nicoll, Maurice. *Psychological Commentaries on The Teachings of Gurdjieff and Ouspensky, Vol I.* Boulder/London: Shambhala, 1984.

Nikhilananda, Swami. *An Inquiry into the Nature of the Seer and the Seen.* Mysore: Sri Ramakrishna Ashrama, 1976.

Nisargadatta Maharaj. *I Am That, Volume I.* Bombay: Chetana, 1978.

_____. *I Am That, Volume II.* Bombay: Chetana, 1978.

Osistynski, Wikton. *Contrasts: Soviet and American Thinkers Discuss the Future.*

Peat, F. David. *Synchronicity: The Bridge Between Matter and Mind.* New York: Bantam Books, 1987.

_____ and Briggs, John. *The Turbulent Mirror: An Illustrated Guide to Chaos Theory & the Science of Wholeness.* New York: Harper & Row, 1989.

_____. *Einstein's Moon: Bell's Therom and the Curious Quest for Quantum Reality.* Chicago: Contempary Books, 1990.

_____. *The Philosopher's Stone: Chaos, Synchronicity, and the Hidden Order of the World.* New York: Bantam Books, 1991.

Poddar, Hanumanprasad. *The Philosophy of Love.* Rajgangur: Orissa, 1978.

Pradhan, V.G. *Janaeshvari: A Song-Sermon on the Bhagavad Gita, Volume I.* Bombay: Blackie & Sons, 1979.

_____. *Janaeshvari: A Song-Ssermon on the Bhagavad Gita, Volume II.* Bombay: Blackie & Sons, 1979.

Rabten, Geshe. *Echoes of Voidness.* London: Wisdom Publications, 1983.

Ramananda, Swami. *Tripura Rahasya.* Tirusannamali, S. India: Sri Ramanashram, 1980.

Rawson, Philip. *The Art of Tantra.* New York/Toronto: Oxford University Press, 1978.

Reich, Wilhelm. *The Function of the Orgasm. The Discovery of the Orgone.* New York: World Publishing, 1942.

Rossi, Ernest. *The Psychology of Mind Body Healing,* New York: W.W. Norton, 1986.

Russell, Bertrand. *The ABC of Relativity.* New York: New American Library, 1958.

Sadhu, Om. *The Path of Sri Ramana.* Kerala, India: Sri Ramana Trust, 1981.

Shah, Idries, *A Perfumed Scorpion,* New York: Harper & Row, 1978.

Singh, Jaideva. *Siva Sutra, The Yoga of Supreme Identity.* Delhi: Motilal Banarsidass, 1979.

_____. *Spanda Karikas.* Delhi: Motilal Banarsidass, 1980.

_____. *Vijnanabhairava or Divine Consciousness.* Delhi: Motilal Banarsidass, 1979.

_____. *Pratyabhijnahrdeyam: The Secret of Self Recognition.* Delhi: Motilal Banarsidass. 1963.

Stapp, H., *Nuovo Climento,* 40B, 1977.

Suzuki, P.T. *Zen Buddhism.* New York: Doubleday Anchor Books, 1956.

Suzuki, Shunru. *Zen Mind, Beginner's Mind.* New York: Weatherhill, 1970.

Talbot, Michael. *Mysticism and the New Physics.* New York: Bantam Books, 1981.

_____. *Beyond The Quantum.* New York: Bantam Books, 1987.

_____. *The Holographic Universe.* New York: Harper Collins, 1991.

Toben, Bob and Wolf, Fred. *Space-Time and Beyond: Toward An Explanation of the Unexplainable.* New York: Bantam Books, 1976.

Tulku, Tarthang. *Time, Space and Knowledge: A New Vision of Reality.* Oakland, CA: Dharma Publishing, 1977.

_____. *Hidden Mind of Freedom.* Oakland, CA: Dharma Publishing, 1981.

_____. *Love of Knowledge.* Oakland, CA: Dharma Publishing, 1987.

_____. *Knowledge of Time and Space.* Oakland, CA: Dharma Publishing, 1990.

Venkatesananda, Swami. *The Supreme Yoga.* Western Australia: Chiltern Yoga Trust, 1976. (2 volumes).

Whittaker, Sir Edmond. *Space and Spirit.* Hinsdale, IL: Regnery, 1948

Wilber, Ken, Engler, Jack and Brown, Daniel. *Transformation In Consciousness: Conventional and Contemplative Perspectives on Development.* Boston: New Science Library, Shambhala, 1986.

Wilber, Ken. *No Boundary: Eastern and Western Approaches to Personal Growth.* Boulder/London: New Science Library, Shambhala, 1981.

_____. *Quantum Questions.* Boston: New Science Library, Shambhala, 1984.

Wilson, Colin. *G.I. Gurdjieff: The War Against Sleep.* England: Aquarian Press, 1980.

Wittgenstein, Ludwig. *Tractatus Logico-Philosophicus.* Great Britian: Routledge & Kegan Paul, Ltd., 1961.

Wolf, Fred Alan. *Taking the Quantum Leap: the New Physics for Nonscientists.* New York: Harper & Row, 1981.

_____. *Space, Time and Beyond.* New York: Bantam, 1983.

_____. *Star Wave: Mind, Consciousness, and Quantum Physics.* New York: Macmillan, 1984.

_____. *Parallel Universes: the Search for Other Worlds.* New York: Touchstone Books, Simon & Schuster, Inc., 1988.

Wolinsky, Stephen H. *Trances People Live: Healing Approaches in Quantum Psychology*. Norfolk, CT: Bramble Co., 1991.

_____. *The Tao of Chaos: Quantum Consciousness, Volume II*. Forthcoming.

Zukav, Gary. *The Dancing Wu Li Masters: An Overview of the New Physics*. New York: Bantam Books, 1984.

INDEX

Lightning Source UK Ltd.
Milton Keynes UK
UKOW02f1926270516

275135UK00001B/34/P